Englisch für berufliche Schulen

2nd edition

Do it! ADVANCED

von

Chris Caridia

unter Mitarbeit der Verlagsredaktion

Cornelsen

Do it! ADVANCED

Englisch für berufliche Schulen
2nd edition

Verfasser: Chris Caridia
Beraterinnen: Stefanie Geyer; Julia Gieger, Jessica van Beeck
Projektleitung: Andreas Goebel
Verlagsredaktion: Kari-ann Warnakulasuriya
Außenredaktion: Joanne Popp, editing etc.
Redaktionelle Mitarbeit: Oliver Busch (Wörterverzeichnisse), Simone Neumann, Louise Turner
Layout: zweiband.media, Berlin
Technische Umsetzung: Straive
Umschlaggestaltung: Ungermeyer – grafische Angelegenheiten, Berlin
Titelfoto: Shutterstock / Dragon Images
Illustrationen: D'Avila Illustration Agency

Erhältlich sind auch:
Schülerbuch – Lehrerfassung mit Lösungen, Audio-CD und Zusatzmaterialien online ISBN 978-3-06-452242-8

www.cornelsen.de

1. Auflage, 1. Druck 2021

Alle Drucke dieser Auflage sind inhaltlich unverändert und können im Unterricht nebeneinander verwendet werden.

Druck und Bindung: Mohn Media Mohndruck, Gütersloh

ISBN 978-3-06-452215-2 (Schülerbuch)
ISBN 978-3-06-452240-4 (E-Book)

PEFC
PEFC/04-31-1033

PEFC zertifiziert
Dieses Produkt stammt aus nachhaltig bewirtschafteten Wäldern und kontrollierten Quellen.

www.pefc.de

Contents

Auf einen Blick

Do it! 2nd edition Advanced eignet sich besonders für den Unterricht im zweiten Jahr der Berufsfachschule oder anderen beruflichen Bildungsgängen auf Niveau A2/B1. Das Lehrwerk kann für sich oder als Aufbaustufe von Do it! A1/A2 benutzt werden, um die Anforderungen der zweijährigen BFS insbesondere mit beruflichen Themen optimal abzudecken. Es enthält Materialien auf Stufe A2-B1 des Gemeinsamen europäischen Referenzrahmens.

So finden Sie sich im Buch zurecht:

Warm up: Jede Unit beginnt mit einer Einstiegsseite, die kommunikativ in das Thema einführt.

Parts: Auf diesen Doppelseiten werden lebensnahe Inhalte und Themen mit interessanten Texten, abwechslungsreichen Aufgaben und vielen Sprechanlässen behandelt. Eine große Vielfalt an Differenzierungsaufgaben, die mit diesen Symbolen ☆★ markiert sind und die Sie im Anhang finden, fördern dabei das individualisierte Lernen.

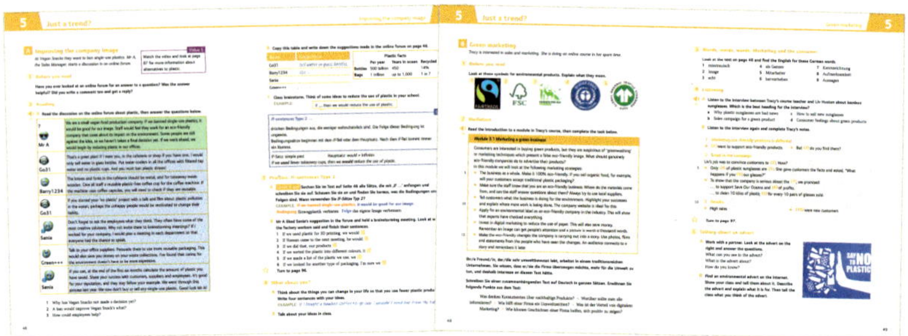

A different perspective: Diese Doppelseite entwickelt ein tieferes Verständnis anderer Perspektiven und interkultureller Unterschiede.

Skills practice: Hier wird die Arbeit an verschiedenen Fertigkeiten explizit geübt und vertieft.

Project: Am Ende einer jeden Unit steht ein handlungsorientiertes Projekt; hier soll mit den erworbenen sprachlichen Fertigkeiten ein haptisches Produkt erstellt werden. Außerdem kann man mit Hilfe des *Snapshot*-Kästchens über das Gelernte selbst reflektieren.

Videos: Kurze Videos beleuchten einzelne Aspekte der Units aus einem anderen Blickwinkel. Übungen dazu sind im Anhang zu finden.

Anhang: Außerdem finden Sie *Partner files, Differentiation files, Grammar summary* und Wörterverzeichnisse.

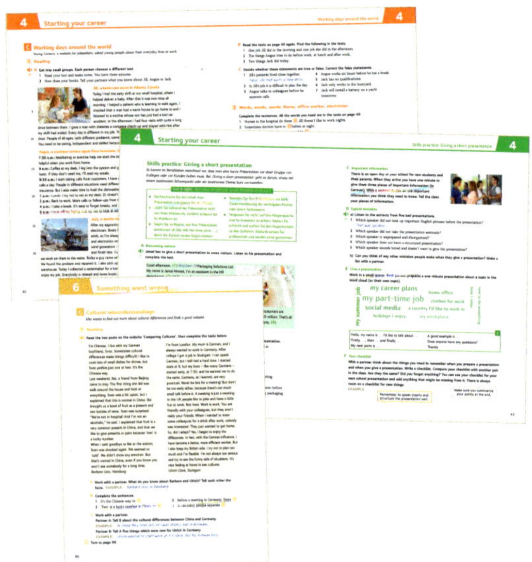

Die Symbole 🔊 und 🎬 verweisen auf die Audio- und Videomaterialien, die Sie in der Lehrerfassung finden. Die Übungen zu den Videos befinden sich im Anhang.

Lehrerfassung: Die praktische Lehrerfassung des Buches bietet Lösungen direkt auf der Seite und zeigt neue Vokabeln an. Außerdem gibt es viele nützliche Zusatzmaterialien wie Kopiervorlagen und Differenzierungsblätter, die per Webcode abrufbar sind.

Viel Spaß beim Lernen und gutes Gelingen wünschen Ihnen Autor und Verlag!

Student jobs 1

Warm-up: Friends around the world

A **Last summer Tracy, Jamal and Mia worked on a farm in Cornwall. Read the ad. Choose the best two jobs for each person.**

Name: Tracy (18)
From: Liverpool
Studies: IT and computing
Interests: Repairing cars; sport; fitness

Name: Jamal (18)
From: Toronto
Studies: Business
Interests: Cooking and food; music

Name: Mia (17)
From: Cologne
Studies: Health and social care
Interests: Young children; horse riding

Working holidays in the UK

Our farm is in beautiful Cornwall. It has holiday flats, group rooms and a restaurant. We offer tennis and horse riding for children and adults.

We need students to help:

- in the kitchen and restaurant.
- look after the children.
- with farm work (need to be fit and strong).
- at reception.
- care for the horses.
- check and repair the farm machines.

B **Why do a summer job? Write down what is important for you and then discuss with your partner. Number your priorities: 1 (important) – 6 (not important).**

Summer jobs are good for young people because they can …

- earn money.
- travel.
- learn about the world of work.
- meet new people.
- do something useful.
- *(your own ideas)*

C **Tell the class about your list.**

EXAMPLE:

Birgit and I both agree that money is the most important reason.

I think that the second most important thing is ... but Mark doesn't agree with me.

A Work experience

Tracy, Jamal and Mia became friends on the farm in Cornwall, and they still keep in touch.

1 Before you read

What internship or voluntary job would you like to do? Discuss your ideas with a partner.

2 Reading

2 **Read the texts, then complete the tasks below.**

Group chat: Cornwall friends

Tracy Black Hey there. You know I told you I need to earn some money to buy a car? Well, yesterday I had an interview for a Saturday job, in a bike workshop. They are really busy and they need someone to help with servicing and repairing the bikes, especially the new e-bikes. I don't need to be a qualified mechanic, but I have to be good with my hands and practical. I always repair bikes, so I have some experience. They pay by the hour, which is OK. I think the interview went well. I'll hear on Monday if I got it.

Mia Nowak You are their best choice!

Jamal Saleh Hope they offer it to you. Yesterday I finished my internship. I have to write a short report. The beginning is attached. What do you think?

Hi Jamal and Tracy,

Sorry I haven't been in touch. I started a new job three weeks ago; I'm a volunteer in a refugee centre. The refugees have so many great stories – they aren't all sad. Two evenings a week I teach basic German and help people to fill in forms or translate letters for them. They ask me what to say on the phone in German too. Everyone finds that really difficult. I have the same problems in English!

I work in the café at the centre on Saturdays or do activities with the young kids. My mum always bakes a cake for me to take there. I'm learning all about Syrian food from a refugee, Jamal!

Take care,

Mia

Internship report

Packaging Solutions Ltd. in Toronto is a young high-tech company which produces packaging for medicine. The packaging saves energy and is easy to transport. I'm interested in design and I liked what I read about the company's programme for students.

I worked in four different departments – Design, Production, Sales and Human Resources. In each department a member of staff explained their job to me. I also had tasks to do by myself.

The internship was very useful. I have experienced what it is like to work in a large organization. The tasks I had were often difficult, but they really helped me to understand the work better.

A Match a picture to each text. There is one more picture than you need.

1

2

3

4

B Complete the sentences.

1 Yesterday Tracy
2 During his internship, Jamal worked in
3 Mia teaches the refugees German and

☆ ★ **Turn to page 93.**

> **!** *to spend*: money or time
>
> I **spent too long** in the shop.
> I **spent €200**.

3 Discussion

A You have arrived in a new country. You don't know anything about it or speak the language. Join the phrases below to make questions to ask someone from the country. Write them down.

How do I …	learn your language?
What do I need to …	open a bank account?
What is a/the …	find a job?
Where can I …	meet people?
	look for a flat?
	buy food?
	typical food in your country?
	weather like in summer/winter?

B Work with a partner and answer the questions for Germany.

G Word order

Subjekt + Verb + Objekt	Ort + Zeit	Adverb + Verb
I enjoy my job.	*We went* ***to the UK last year****.*	*They* ***often chat****.*
Do ***you like your work?***	*Did you meet* ***on a farm in May****?*	*Mia* ***almost forgot****.*
		Aber nach *to be*:
		It ***is usually*** *on a Sunday.*

4 Practice: Word order

A Check it out! Suchen Sie je einen Satz in den Texten auf Seite 6 mit:

1 Subjekt + Verb + Objekt
2 Ort vor Zeit
3 Adverb vor einem Hauptverb
4 Adverb nach einer Form von *to be*

B Put the words in the right order and write complete sentences.

1 German | Mia | teaches | always | on Thursday evenings.
2 likes | in the classroom | early. | She | to arrive
3 already | was | Yesterday | there. | one student
4 had | The student | the next day. | in a factory | a job interview
5 was | often | in class. | very nervous | The student
6 "I | friends | don't | usually | Mia said, | call | late."

B Finding an internship

Tracy wants to do an internship. She asks Jamal about his internship in Toronto in a group video call.

1 Before you read

Look at the pictures. Where would you like to do an internship? Discuss with a partner.

L

I'd prefer to …
If I could, I'd like to …
… doesn't really interest me.
I can't decide if …

2 Reading

Read the dialogue and complete the tasks below.

3

Mia: That was my week. Next week I get my exam results. I hope I didn't fail!

Tracy: Cool, Mia. I'm sure you passed. Hey, I need your help guys.

Mia: Sure. What's up?

Tracy: Well, I've found a vocational college where I can train as a computer technician. What I need now is an internship. I'm not sure where to start. Could you tell me about yours, Jamal? How did you get it?

Jamal: It wasn't easy. Companies prefer students from universities, not high schools. I wrote to ten companies, saying: *I am a high-school student with a great interest in … I am writing to discuss the possibility of …*. I had two interviews, and one company offered me an internship. Try family contacts or ask the students in your class.

Mia: What about the interviews?

Jamal: I found out about the companies on the internet. I wore a dark business suit, not just my black jeans. They weren't online interviews either.

Tracy: That sounds cool. I can see why you got the job! How about the work? What was your typical day like?

Jamal: Every morning there was a meeting for the group I was working in. I didn't really understand much anyone said. But later my mentor explained things. Lunch in the company cafeteria was great, even for vegetarians like me. And it wasn't expensive. On Fridays, there was 'Learn with Lunch', when a highly-qualified member of staff talked to us about his or her work. That was really interesting, and I learned a lot. At the end we all got certificates. They even offered apprenticeships to two interns.

Tracy: I hope I find a company like that.

Jamal: I'm sure you will. But when I left the office at 5 o'clock, you'll never guess what I enjoyed most. The beautiful green park around the office building. I felt that I could breathe again!

Mia: I know just what you mean.

!

as good/big/tasty **as** that = *so … wie*

A Which is the best answer, a, b or c? Jamal talks about …

- **a** what he did after work every day.
- **b** how he found his internship and what he did there.
- **c** the jobs the other interns did.

B Decide whether these statements are true or false. Correct the false statements.

1. Tracy has found an internship.
2. Jamal wrote to a lot of companies before he found an internship.
3. Before the interviews, he learned all about the companies.
4. Some days began with a morning meeting.
5. 'Learn with Lunch' took place on Wednesdays.
6. Jamal was always happy to leave the office building.

Video 1
Watch the video and look at page 85 for more ideas about how to find an internship.

3 Words, words, words: Qualifications

A Find the English words in the text for these German ones.

1 Praktikanten	4 Ausbildung	7 (eine Prüfung) bestehen
2 hochqualifiziert	5 Zeugnis	8 (bei einer Prüfung) durchfallen
3 Berufsschule	6 Prüfungsergebnisse	9 eine Ausbildung zum ... machen

☆ ★ **Turn to page 93.**

B Complete the sentences with your answers in A.

1. Mia is very nervous about the ___ that she will get next week.
2. Students need more than 70% to ___ the test.
3. An ___ in the company lasts for three years.
4. Students at college can do a ___ which gives them practical training for work.
5. She studied for five years, so she is ___ .

4 Listening

Listen to five students talk about their internships, then complete the tasks below.

4 **A Who said it? Match the interns (1–5) with their statements (a–f). There is one statement more than you need.**

- **a** I asked lots of questions.
- **b** I just watched and tried to understand the job.
- **c** The most important thing was to use what I learned in class.
- **d** I have experience of work in different organizations.
- **e** I really understood how teams work together.
- **f** I learned about a job that I didn't like.

B Listen again. Which of the interns (1–5) was it?

- **a** Who didn't ask many questions?
- **b** Who didn't feel excited at the end of the internship?
- **c** Who did more than one internship?
- **d** Who worked in a factory?
- **e** Who has just applied for a job?
- **f** Who had lots of questions?
- **g** Who was with one person for a whole day?
- **h** Who made friends with other interns?

C Leaving college

Bill Hearn has an IT business in Liverpool. Here he is talking about his experience.

1 Mediation

5

Read what Bill Hearn said, then complete the tasks below.

Things I didn't know when I left college …

It's your life and your decisions. Take your time to think about your future. You don't have to do what your friends or classmates do. Your parents' ideas for you may be quite different to your real interests. My parents wanted me to follow a 'safe' career in hotel management like my sister. I tried it for three years. It's okay to change your career plans though, you just need to start somewhere. I decided to follow my own dreams and started my own company.

Learn how to manage your money. At college I didn't need to worry much about money. And nobody taught me anything about it. When I left college, I had to learn fast how to pay bills and save my money. I did some silly things and found myself with a big overdraft. It took me three years to pay it back. I couldn't afford a holiday or a car in that time.

Never give up. That's another hard lesson I learned. If you can't get the job you want, make a plan. Maybe there are alternatives which are better. My exam results in college were not good and I didn't get any interviews for the jobs I applied for. I was so frustrated that I gave up and did what my parents wanted me to do.

When I left college, I thought, "Great, no more homework!" But I was very wrong. My education has never stopped. I learn new things every day. We are on a journey all our lives. "The person who graduates today and stops learning tomorrow is uneducated the day after." That's a quote I found on the internet and liked.

The final thing I didn't know was how little time I had. Between school and work and paying those bills, I worried about my future, I planned, and I researched. I never relaxed and enjoyed the present moment. And nobody told me to stop. So, enjoy your summer holidays and your free time. Do something new. You may remember it all your life.

A Arbeiten Sie zu fünft. Jede Person liest einen Teil des Textes und berichtet der Gruppe auf Deutsch, worum es in ihrem Teil geht.

B Schreiben Sie für die Website der Schule einen zusammenhängenden Text auf Deutsch über Bills Erfahrungen. Erwähnen Sie folgende Punkte:

- Was sollte man bei Entscheidungen über den zukünftigen Beruf bedenken?
- Welche finanziellen Schwierigkeiten hatte Bill, nachdem er die Schule verlassen hatte, und warum?
- Was sollte man machen, wenn Bewerbungen nicht erfolgreich sind?
- Wann hört Bildung auf?
- Wie sollte man die Zeit zwischen Schule und Beruf nutzen?

☆★ **Turn to page 93.**

2 Words, words, words: Job choices

Complete the career advisor's questions with the words in the box.

desk ▪ goals ▪ numbers ▪ income ▪ satisfaction ▪ search
on-the-job ▪ outdoor ▪ register

1 Did you make a list of your ___? Where do you want to be in five years?
2 Which is more important to you, a high ___ or job ___?
3 Are you good with your hands or good at ___?
4 Do you prefer a ___ job in front of a computer or an ___ job?
5 Do you want a job with ___ training or would you like to study?
6 Did you ___ on a website and do a job ___?

G

Simple present		Simple past	
I/you/we/they work.	He/she/it work**s**.	I/you/he/she/it/we/they work**ed**.	
Do you work?	Do**es** he work?	Did you work?	**Did** he work?
You don't work.	He do**esn't** work.	You didn't work.	He **didn't** work.

3 Practice: Simple present and simple past

Complete the message with the verbs in brackets. Use the simple present or the simple past.

Hey Mike,
Greetings from Florida! Sorry, I (1) (not/have) time to tell you about our trip before we left. A group of us (2) (decide) it's the best way to celebrate finishing college before we start our apprenticeships. We all (3) (find) apprenticeships a few weeks ago. (4) (I/tell) you I wanted an apprenticeship in a hotel?
Anyway, Miami is amazing! The city just (5) (not/sleep). We (6) (not have) much money, but there are lots of students where we are staying. The beach (7) (not/cost) anything and it (8) (not/get) cold here at night. What are you up to?
Gabi

4 Pairwork: A role play

A You and your partner plan to spend the summer in the UK. Read the three alternatives that you have found on the internet.

Fruit picking, Scotland	Volunteer jobs, Manchester	Holidays for students, Cornwall
• Fair wages • Mon-Fri 8 hours a day; Sat 5 hours • Meet lots of people • Beautiful mountain area	• Serve customers with a smile • Help clean the shop • 4 hours a day, 5 days a week • Free accommodation in the summer!	• Warm climate • Beautiful beaches • Ideal for surfing • Early or late summer for best prices

B Partner A go to file 1 on page 89. Partner B go to file 10 on page 92. Read your profile, then agree on one of the alternatives in A.

Skills practice: Breaking the ice

Es kommt im Beruf häufig vor, dass man mit fremden Menschen ins Gespräch kommen muss. Oft weiß man nicht, wie man in solchen Situationen ein Gespräch anfangen soll. Hier finden Sie einige Hilfestellungen für diese Situationen.

Get it right: *Wie fange ich ein Gespräch mit fremden Menschen an?*

- Bedenken Sie, dass die meisten Menschen bei einer Veranstaltung wenige Leute kennen – so wie Sie.
- Versuchen Sie, an Unterhaltungen teilzunehmen. Stellen Sie sich vor und fragen Sie, ob Sie teilnehmen dürfen.
- Gehen Sie langsam umher, suchen Sie Augenkontakt, lächeln und zeigen Sie damit, dass Sie für eine Unterhaltung offen sind.
- Beginnen Sie ein Gespräch am Buffet über die angebotenen Getränke und Speisen.
- Sagen Sie etwas über die Räumlichkeiten oder die Veranstaltung an sich.
- Vermeiden Sie negative Bemerkungen.
- Englisch ist nicht Ihre Muttersprache: Das ist ein gutes Thema, ein Gespräch zu beginnen.
- Themen wie Sport oder das Wetter, die für Smalltalk gut geeignet sind, sind weniger gut zu Beginn eines Gesprächs.

A Good or bad topics?

Discuss with a partner. Which of these topics could you use to start a conversation? Which are not good topics? Explain why in German.

1 where you come from
2 if the other person knows many people
3 the bad food
4 the weather
5 the company you work for
6 part of the event you're looking forward to
7 sport
8 how bored you are
9 how interesting the event is
10 your bad English

B Starting a conversation

Match the beginnings (1–6) with the right endings (a–f).

1 Are you enjoying
2 Excuse me, do you mind
3 Do you know
4 Was that your first
5 This coffee
6 That was a good presentation,

a many people here?
b presentation at this company?
c is just what I need!
d the presentations?
e don't you think?
f if I join you?

C Listen to the conversation

6

Fill in the gaps with sentences A–J. There is one more sentence than you need.

Angela: (1)
Chris: Yes, they are tasty. I've just eaten two!
Angela: I'll try one. (2) in your coffee? Where are you standing? (3)
Chris: Of course. I'm just over here.
Angela: Thanks. My name is Angela Blum.
Chris: I'm Chris Baker.
Angela: (4)
Chris: Yes, it was very useful. I learned a lot. But it's good to have a break now.
Angela: (5)
Chris: No, it's my third one actually.
Angela: (6)
Chris: Not really. Only a few.
Angela: (7) Everybody has to get home.
Chris: Yes, it takes me an hour to get home.
Angela: (8) I'm a trainee. I started at the beginning of September.
Chris: Really? Sorry, I think the next talk starts soon and I need to go to G4.
Angela: Me too! (9)

- **A** Did you enjoy the talk just now?
- **B** I see from your name tag that you're in the software department.
- **C** I suppose there's no time to socialize after the event.
- **D** Is it OK if I join you?
- **E** Is this your first training course?
- **F** Are you alone here?
- **G** So, you must know a lot of people.
- **H** Those little cakes look good, don't they?
- **I** We can walk there together.
- **J** Would you like some milk

D Ending a conversation

Complete the polite ways to end a conversation with a stranger. Use the words in the box.

business card ▪ email ▪ excuse ▪ nice ▪ make ▪ maybe ▪ seen

I've just (1) someone I need to speak to. It was very (2) to meet you. (3) we can talk later.

If you'll (4) me, I have to (5) a phone call. Do you have a (6)? I can (7) you next week.

E Pairwork: A role play

On a training course you don't know anybody. In the break you have ten minutes to get to know some of the people. Start and finish short conversations with three people in your class.

Project page: Survey of your class's career plans

You are going to do a short survey of your classmates' plans when they leave school.

A **Divide the class into four groups. Each group takes a different survey question from the four on the right.**

B **Each person in your group answers your question. One person writes down the answers.**

C **Ask the people in the other three groups your question and write down their answers.**

D **Prepare the results of your survey. You can use a bar chart or pie charts.**

E **Present the results.**

L

Our results show …
It's surprising that …
Most of the class thinks that …
A few people knew …
Everybody has …
Some people gave other answers.
For example, …

Survey questions

1 When people ask you about your career plans, what do you think?
- **a** I'm bored.
- **b** I don't have enough information yet.
- **c** I'm excited to talk about my plans.
- **d** *give another answer*

2 Do you know what type of career you are interested in?
- **a** Yes, I'm 100 percent sure.
- **b** There are 2-3 I'm interested in.
- **c** I have no idea.
- **d** *give another answer*

3 Which of the following have you done?
- **a** Talked to parents, teachers and friends.
- **b** Looked at websites about careers.
- **c** Done an internship.
- **d** *give another answer*

4 What are your plans for the first two months when you leave college?
- **a** Stay at home or go on a holiday.
- **b** Find a summer job.
- **c** Go to a summer school.
- **d** *give another answer*

F **Give the other groups feedback on their presentation. Look at page 100 for some useful feedback phrases.**

Snapshot

What was your favourite thing in this unit?

What important thing did you learn?

What do you need to work on?

Job applications 2

Warm-up: Choosing a career

A Which vocational areas do pictures 1-8 belong to?

Business training ▪ Construction ▪ Health and social care
Childcare ▪ Technical training ▪ Travel and tourism
Hair and beauty ▪ Hotel and catering

3

4

5

6

7

8

1

2

B Match these skills with what some applicants said. There is one skill per comment (1–8).

communicates well ▪ confident ▪ leader ▪ motivated
organized ▪ team player ▪ understands business
can work under pressure

1 I can explain things well.
2 I volunteer with a team of firefighters.
3 I'm the captain of my football team.
4 I enjoy selling things on the internet.
5 I write a 'to-do' list with the things I have to do every day.
6 I wanted to go to the USA, so I got a part-time job.
7 I had to work fast in my job in a restaurant.
8 I don't have problems presenting things to a big group.

C Which of the skills from B have you got?

EXAMPLE:

Before a test I study all weekend.

I don't like being late.

2 Job applications

A Finding out about careers

Tracy, Jamal and Mia have looked at different careers on the internet. Tracy is interested in IT.

1 Before you read

Would you like a job working with computers and IT? Why (not)?

2 Reading

7 **Read this information from a school leavers website, then complete the tasks below.**

What does a career in IT mean?
Typical jobs in IT involve helping organizations buy hardware and software that is best for their needs or giving them technical support. Your business skills should be as good as your technical skills. Find out more about possible IT careers:

developing websites	testing software	cyber security
developing networks	technical sales	IT support

What are the most important skills and personal qualities you need for a career in IT?
An interest in technology. This is the most important and will keep you motivated.
Good at maths. A lot of IT jobs need maths.
Attention to detail. A mistake in a code can cause bigger problems than you think!
Open to life-long learning. Technology changes fast – learning doesn't finish after college.
Good at teamwork. A lot of jobs are projects where you work with colleagues in a team.
Work long hours. IT work, such as updating a network, is often done outside office hours.

A The information about IT careers is in two parts. Tell your partner what each part is about.

B True or false? Correct the false statements.

1. Business skills are important for IT jobs.
2. Technical support for organizations is the most typical area for IT jobs.
3. You are always learning new things in an IT career.
4. Teamwork is important because you work outside the office.

3 Listening

8 **A Listen to Aiya, Tracy's cousin. Put the information (a–d) in the order you hear it (1–4).**

- **a** She was nervous at the beginning.
- **b** She now has a permanent job.
- **c** She didn't know what to do after college.
- **d** She was motivated and well prepared.

B Listen again and complete the sentences.

1. Aiya's brother works in IT and he ___
2. At the start everybody knew Aiya was an apprentice, so ___
3. Aiya always asked questions and never ___
4. ___ a team of ten people.

☆ ★ **Turn to page 93/94.**

G

Adjectives ...

machen Ihre Texte interessanter.
Man steigert sie mit *-er/-est* oder *more/most*.

!

I have a job and ten colleagues.
I have an **exciting** job and **the best** colleagues.

	Adjektiv	Komparativ	Superlativ
eine Silbe	*long, big*	*long**er**, big**ger***	*(the) long**est**, big**gest***
zwei Silben mit **-y**	*lucky*	*luck**ier***	*(the) luck**iest***
zwei und mehr Silben	*important*	***more** important*	*(the) **most** important*
unregelmäßig	*good*	*better*	*(the) best*
	bad	*worse*	*(the) worst*

4 Practice: Comparative and superlative of adjectives

A Check it out! **Suchen Sie je einen Satz im Text auf Seite 16 mit:**

1 einem unregelmäßigen Superlativ
2 einem einsilbigen Adjektiv im Komparativ
3 einem mehrsilbigen Adjektiv im Superlativ

B Complete the sentences with the comparative or superlative of the adjectives in brackets.

1 After he left college, Lawrence wanted to go on the ___ holiday he had ever been on. (long)
2 "It will be ___ to find a job in October," he told his girlfriend. (easy)
3 "Summer is ___ time to find a job because everybody is on holiday." (bad)
4 "I'll be ___ if we go away after we find jobs." (happy)
5 "OK, then let's go on ___ holiday that we can afford." (beautiful)

5 Mediation

9

Mia überlegt sich, eine Stelle als Erzieherin im Ausland zu suchen. Lesen Sie Olivers Blog, den Mia gefunden hat. Notieren Sie Olivers Tätigkeiten und ergänzen Sie die Uhrzeiten, wann er was macht.

Olivers Aufgaben: 7:00 Arbeitsbeginn

I start work at the nursery school at 7 a.m. The rooms are quiet, but soon parents and children begin arriving. At 8:30 we all eat a healthy breakfast together. I sit with the children, talk to them and help them if they need it. After breakfast, at 9 o'clock, we welcome the day and sing our favourite songs. The group sits in a big circle on the floor and I play my guitar. The children love it. The rest of the morning we do fun learning activities in groups. Some of the children do arts and crafts and others do science and discovery. Lunch is at 12 o'clock. We like the children behaving well at the table. There is an hour of quiet time at 1 o'clock. I sit in a corner and read to a group of children. Some of them fall asleep. At 2, there's a snack and then everyone goes out to the playground to play in the fresh air. Parents arrive at 3 o'clock to collect their tired children but I still have office work to do: there's a parents' evening next week. At 5 o'clock I finish work at the nursery school and cycle home to my own children.

B Answering a job ad

Jamal finds this interesting ad for a job at Packaging Solutions Ltd., where he did his internship.

1 Reading

Read the job advertisement, then complete the task below.

Human Resources Assistant

Packaging Solutions Ltd. is a global leader in packaging for medicines. Our head office in Toronto is looking for an assistant to support our HR managers.

Responsibilities:

- Help job applicants and employees
- Organize training courses
- Prepare reports for French-Canadian clients
- Keep files and records up to date
- Experience with computers and Microsoft Word
- Check the references on job applications

Requirements:

- Diploma in business administration or similar
- Good communication skills
- Organizational skills
- Attention to detail
- Post job vacancies
- Bilingual

Send your application to: Ms Marie Leblanc

1 One of the responsibilities and one of the requirements are in the wrong list. Which ones?
2 Which responsibilities go best with which requirements? Match them.
3 What other requirements are there for an HR assistant job? Discuss with your partner.

2 A covering letter

Read Jamal's covering letter and complete the tasks on the next page.

10

Dear Ms Leblanc,

I would like to apply for the position of Human Resources Assistant as advertised on your company website.

Last summer I did an internship in your office in Toronto, so I know your organization. Packaging Solutions Ltd. is developing exciting new ways of packaging medicines and it is growing fast. I would like to be part of this success. I am hard-working and a good organizer and communicator. My computer skills are excellent.

I have just completed my Diploma in Business Administration with focus on HR. I have a strong interest in employees and their employment and I would like a career in HR now I'm qualified.

I enclose my CV with full details of my qualifications and the part-time work that I have done.

I would welcome the opportunity to discuss the position further.

I look forward to hearing from you.

Yours sincerely,

Jamal Ahmed

A Choose the correct answer.

1 Jamal read the ad	a in a newspaper.	b online.	c in an email.
2 Jamal has good	a computer skills.	b language skills.	c people skills.
3 Jamal wants a career in	a packaging.	b administration.	c human resources.
4 He sends Ms Leblanc his	a work.	b HR.	c CV.

B Which five things does Jamal write about in his covering letter?

1 the job he is applying for
2 the salary he wants
3 the skills he has for the job
4 useful experience he doesn't have
5 the documents he is enclosing
6 why he is applying
7 where he read about the job
8 a list of his certificates and qualifications

Turn to page 94.

3 Words, words, words: Verbs, nouns and adjectives

A Copy and complete the table with the correct forms. You can find the words on page 18.

Verb	Noun	Noun (person)	Adjective
employ			
organize			
communicate			
qualify			

B Complete the sentences. Use the verbs in brackets and the right form from your table in A.

1 I found as an intern in the London office. (employ)
2 I am a mechanic. (qualify)
3 I know I can use my skills. (organize)
4 It is better if our is via email. (communicate)

> **!**
> to apply **for** a job
> to communicate **with** sb
> to qualify **in** a subject
> to look forward **to** (hear)**ing**

4 Pairwork: Information gap activity

Find the missing parts (1–10) from the email. Partner A goes to file 2 on page 89 and reads parts (a–j). Then partner B reads the email aloud. Partners A and B agree on the missing part for each gap.

I am writing to apply for the job of video game tester (1)
I am 19 years old, (2) I am very familiar with all the top video games on the market and well qualified to work on new games. I believe my qualifications (3)
My technical skills are excellent. I have taken coding courses and I have a web design qualification. I am currently (4) I am highly motivated, (5) used to working late at night. I am also an experienced team player. The games I take part in (6) (7) details and a list of the popular games which I know very well. I understand that your offices are in California. This is not a problem because I (8) for a video interview.
I feel that (9) and would fit well in your testing team. I hope that you will give me (10)

C Comparing CVs

Mia and Tracy are looking at their CVs before they apply for jobs.

Video 2

Watch the video and look at page 85 for more information about choosing the right career.

1 Reading

Compare the two CVs with a partner. Partner A looks at the CV below and partner B looks at the CV in file 4 on page 90. Then complete the task below.

Persönliche Daten

Name	Mia Nowak
Geburtsdatum	16.09.200_
Geburtsort	Hannover
Anschrift	Luftstr. 2, 51105 Köln
E-Mail	m.nowak@yxz.dex
Telefon	0151 12345

Schulbildung

Sept 202_ - Juli 202_	Berufsfachschule (Gesundheit, Erziehung, Soziales), Köln
Sept 201_ - Juli 202_	Anne-Frank-Realschule, Köln

! Die aktuellste Information steht immer oben.

Schulpraktika

Juli 202_	3-wöchiges Praktikum, Caritasverband, Köln
Februar 201_	1-wöchiges Praktikum, Plus Versicherung, Köln

Berufliche Erfahrung

Jan 202_ - (jetzt)	Ehrenamtliche Helferin im Flüchtlingszentrum
August 202_	Arbeitsurlaub auf einem Bauernhof in Großbritannien

Interessen und Kenntnisse

Lieblingsfächer	Biologie, Kunst
Sprachkenntnisse	Englisch (B1), Polnisch (A1)
EDV-Kenntnisse	Microsoft Word
Hobbys	Reiten, Tierschutz

Welche drei Aussagen sind falsch?

1. Im englischen Lebenslauf sind Referenzen verfügbar.
2. Beide Lebensläufe enthalten eine kurze Beschreibung des Bewerbers / der Bewerberin.
3. Fertigkeiten werden nur im englischen Lebenslauf aufgelistet.
4. Ein Foto des Bewerbers / der Bewerberin gibt es nur im deutschen Lebenslauf.
5. Alle Zeiträume stehen rechts im englischen Lebenslauf.
6. Der/Die deutsche Bewerber/in hat Arbeitserfahrung als Teil seiner/ihrer Schulbildung angegeben.
7. Noten und Qualifikationen werden in beiden angegeben.

☆ ★ **Turn to page 94.**

2 Before you listen

Look at the parts of these CVs and discuss with a partner the mistakes the people have made.

1 Personal profile:
Works very good in a team

2 Email:
rock.hero@abc.nex

3 Hobbies and interests:
Computer games
Football
Reading
Birdwatching
Cycling
Films

3 Listening

11

A Listen to the careers advisor talk about mistakes people make in CVs. Put the advisor's tips in the right order (a–g). There is one tip too many.

- **a** It should be clear, simple and easy to find information.
- **b** Don't write long lists.
- **c** Give just one phone number.
- **d** Have an email address which is serious.
- **e** Don't write more than two pages.
- **f** Ask somebody to read your CV.
- **g** Check that the information is still correct.

B Match the keywords with the tips in A. Remember there is one tip too many in A.

1. Personal information
2. CV design
3. Grammar/spelling
4. Telephone
5. Email
6. Hobbies or skills

4 Pairwork: A role play

Partner A helps partner B, who is German, write an English CV.
Partner A: Answer B's questions and tell him/her where the information should go on the CV.
Partner B: Turn to file 5 on page 90. Ask A the questions.

Personal profile ▪ Hobbies and interests ▪ Education ▪ Personal information ▪ Work experience ▪ Key skills

You should put that in/under ...

Where should that go?

That's important. You can write that ...

Where do I write ...?

5 Words, words, words: Job, career or work

Complete the sentences with the correct word: job, career or work.

1. I can't make private phone calls when I'm at ___.
2. He's stopped working now but he had a long ___ in business.
3. I met some friends from ___ last Saturday.
4. He did some ___ for them as a student.
5. Now he has a full-time ___ with the company.
6. She lost her ___ because she made too many mistakes.

!
work = allgemeine Tätigkeiten, im Beruf oder privat
job = eine bestimmte Rolle oder Stelle
career = Beruf/Arbeit, den/die man über längere Zeit ausübt

Skills practice: Emails

Auf dieser Seite sehen wir uns Begriffe und Ausdrücke an, die häufig in E-Mails verwendet werden, um zu lernen, wie wir bessere E-Mails schreiben können.

Get it right: *Wie sieht einer geschäftlichen E-Mail aus?*

- **The structure:** E-Mails sollten eine klare Struktur haben.
- **The language:** Verwenden Sie eine formellere Sprache als in privaten E-Mails. Wenn Sie die Person gut kennen, ist eine weniger formelle Sprache in Ordnung.
- **Subject line:** Diese Zeile macht klar, wovon die E-Mail handelt. So wird es einfacher sein, sie später zu finden.
- **Beginning and ending an email:** Verwenden Sie eine formelle Anrede, wenn Sie die Person nicht kennen. Setzen Sie unter Ihrem Namen Ihre Stelle und den Namen Ihrer Firma. Wenn Sie eine/n Geschäftspartner/in gut kennen, reicht es, wenn Sie Vornamen benutzen.
- **First sentence:** In englischem Schriftverkehr beginnt der Textkörper nach der Anrede mit einem Großbuchstaben.
- **The body of an email:** Beginnen Sie den ersten Satz Ihrer E-Mail immer mit einem großen Buchstaben. Schreiben Sie kurze Absätze.

A Reading

Read the emails and find the English phrases for the German phrases in the box.

die Bestätigung schicken ▪ ich freue mich auf ▪ ich gehe davon aus, dass ...
mehr darüber erfahren ▪ setzen Sie sich bitte mit mir in Verbindung
weitere Einzelheiten ▪ möchten Sie einladen ▪ die Stelle als

Dear Mr Ahmed,
Thank you for your application for the position of HR Assistant. We were impressed by your background and would like to invite you to a video interview to tell you more about the job and to get to know you.
Please let me know which of the following times is suitable, and I will send you the confirmation and further details:
Tuesday, May 27 at 10 a.m.
Wednesday, May 28 at 2 p.m.
If you have any questions, please contact me.
We look forward to meeting you.
Regards,
Marie Leblanc
HR Manager, Packaging Solutions Ltd.

! Write *Ms* when you don't know if a woman is married.

Dear Ms Leblanc,
Thank you for the interview invitation for the position of HR Assistant. I am very interested to learn more about the position.
The best time for me is Tuesday, May 27 at 10 a.m. I understand it will be a video interview and you will send me the details of the link and the password.
I look forward to speaking to you.
Best wishes,
Jamal Ahmed

B Emails

Here are four emails (1–4) which are either to or from the HR Department of Packaging Solutions Ltd. Find the correct email replies (a–c). There is one email without a reply.

1 Dear Ms Lee, Please find attached details of the link and password for your interview on Friday. Let me know if anything is not clear. Good luck! Regards,	**a** Hi Julia, Thank you for choosing me. I'm sorry, but I'm on two weeks' holiday then. Is there an alternative date? Best regards,
2 Hi Jackie, I have some good news for you. You have a place on the training course! It's for two weeks from September 1. I hope that date works for you. Best,	**b** Hi Philip, Sorry, I only wrote down the action points, which I'm sure you remember. But let me know if you'd like me to send them. Best wishes,
3 Dear Mr Demir, Thank you for sending your interview travel expenses. Could you also send the receipts, please? You forgot to attach them. Best regards,	**c** Dear Mr Blake, Thank you for your email. Unfortunately, there was no attachment. Could you send it, please? Best regards,
4 John, Could you send me your notes from the meeting yesterday, please? I have to write the report and I can't find mine! Thanks. Regards,	

In English speaking countries, people often use first names in emails at work. It's important to stay polite. Don't use CAPITALS.

C Pairwork: A role play

Partner A: You start work next week as an apprentice in a company, but you still have some questions. Write a short email to the HR department and ask about these things.

- How many days holiday you get
- If you need a medical check-up
- Where to go on your first day
- (your own question)

Partner B: You work in the HR department. Write a reply to the email from partner A.

L

Dear ..., / Hi ..., / Hello ...,
Thank you for sending me ...
I have a question about ...
I'm not sure ...
Could you let me know ..., please?
Thanks / Thank you for ...
I look forward to ...
Best regards, / Regards, / Best wishes,

Project page: Job ad

You are going to design a job ad.

A **In a group of four decide on a job you want to design a job ad for. Use an idea from the pictures or your own idea. Write the name of your job in the centre of a large sheet of paper.**

business assistant

carpenter

baker

landscape gardener

optician

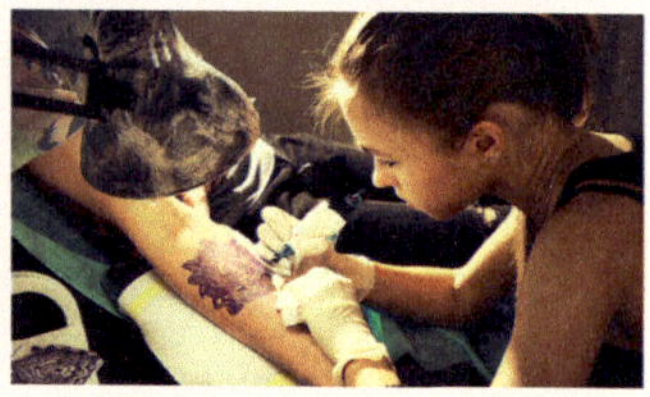

tattoo artist

B **Brainstorm the responsibilities and requirements needed for the job. Research online for more ideas. Divide your piece of paper into four and make notes in your corner of the placemat.**

C **Discuss your ideas with the rest of the group. Agree on six responsibilities and six requirements and write them in the centre of the sheet around the title. Put the responsibilities and requirements in order of importance.**

EXAMPLE:

I think ... is important.

You need to be able to ... for this job.

I don't think ... is necessary.

D **Use your ideas to make a poster for your job ad. Look at the job ad on page 18 to check that you have everything.**

- Keep the text short.
- Write a maximum of six responsibilities and six requirements.
- Don't forget to tell people who to send their CVs to.

E **Do a gallery walk. Give feedback to other groups about their job ads. Which job ad is best? Look at page 100 for some useful feedback phrases.**

Snapshot

What was your favourite thing in this unit?

What important thing did you learn?

What do you need to work on?

Professional life 3

Warm-up: How not to behave at work

A **Match the pictures of wrong behaviour (1–6) with the descriptions in the box. There is one more description than you need.**

late for a meeting ▪ laughing at a colleague ▪ untidy desk
playing online games at work ▪ angry with a colleague
feet on the desk ▪ hair and clothes a mess

1

2

3

4

5

6

B **Now match pictures A–F below with 1–6 above.**

A

B

C

D

E

F

C **With a partner, discuss the correct behaviour.**

EXAMPLE:

It's not friendly to laugh at a colleague. You should always be friendly.

Yes, I agree. How can you work with people if you laugh at them?

L

Giving your opinion

You should (not) …
You ought (not) to …
It's not … to …

3 Professional life

A Making a good impression

Tracy decides she needs to learn more about life at work. She looks for courses online.

1 Before you read

Answer the questions from a quiz in a magazine. Discuss your answers with a partner.

1 You are thinking of getting a tattoo. Where is the best place for it?
- **A** Where everyone can see it.
- **B** Where only your partner can see it.
- **C** Where people can see it when you wear a T-shirt.

2 What is the best definition of being professional?
- **A** Going to work although you feel ill.
- **B** Wearing different clothes every day.
- **C** Always following the boss's rules.

2 Reading

12 **Read this summary of an online course, then complete the tasks on the next page.**

How to be professional at work

I remember your first day as if it was yesterday.

Lesson 1 (1) (25 min)
First impressions are important. You don't get a second chance. People look at you and see how you present yourself. Always dress smartly for work. You should be neat and tidy. Smart is better than casual.

Lesson 2 (2) (20 min)
Remember you are at work to do a job that you get paid for. The company expects you to work hard and be an active member of your team. In meetings, sit up straight, listen carefully, speak directly and clearly, but don't be aggressive or personal. There are times when it is OK to chat quietly to colleagues, but keep it brief. This lesson includes lots of examples of dos and don'ts.

Lesson 3 (3) (35 min)
You don't just communicate with words. Your body, hands, face and eyes also speak for you. They can help you to be successful. We teach you how to show an interest, take things seriously, make eye contact with others and what to do with your hands and arms when you are talking.

Lesson 4 (4) (30 min)
Always answer your work phone quickly and with a polite greeting, and don't forget to say your name. Be friendly, smile and speak clearly. In this lesson, we look at the differences between private and business calls.

Lesson 5 (5) (20 min)
Colleagues are sometimes from different cultures. Body language, for example, can send the wrong signals. In some cultures, it's normal to touch the person you are talking to. In others, it's polite to look down and not look someone in the eye. Learn to show interest and respect for another culture and act appropriately.

A **Choose the missing title for each lesson (1–5). There are two titles that you don't need.**

Giving your best ■ Looking your best ■ Business phone calls
Preparing for a job interview ■ Taking part in meetings ■ Body language
Working with people from other cultures

B **Complete the sentences (1–6) with the correct ending (a–f).**

1 Think carefully about what you wear
2 The way you sit in your chair
3 It's good to be direct and clear, but
4 Work hard and don't
5 On the phone,
6 Body language can be

a speak with a clear and friendly voice.
b don't be aggressive or personal.
c shows you are listening.
d because how you look is important.
e spend too long talking to colleagues.
f different in different cultures.

G

Adjectives and adverbs

Adjectives beschreiben Zustände oder Eigenschaften einer Person oder Sache.
Adverbs beschreiben, wie etwas geschieht und beziehen sich meist auf ein Verb oder ein Adjektiv.

Adjektiv → Adverb

Adjektiv + **-ly**	*quick → quick**ly**; slow → slow**ly***
Adjektiv auf -y > **-ily**	*happy → happ**ily**; easy → eas**ily***
unregelmäßige Adjektive	*good → well; fast → fast; hard → hard; early → early*

3 Practice: Adjectives and adverbs

A **Check it out! Finden Sie fünf Beispiele von Adverbien im Text auf Seite 26.**

B **Complete the sentences with the words in brackets in the correct form.**

1 The new assistant wore some ___ shoes yesterday. (strange)
2 One member of my team speaks quite ___. (aggressive)
3 Watch his body language. It's ___ to guess what he's thinking. (easy)
4 I spoke to her on the phone, but I couldn't understand her very ___. (good)
5 He learned how to do the job ___ and is very popular. (fast)
6 After such a long meeting, I need to find a ___ place to work. (quiet)

☆ ★ **Turn to page 94.**

4 Being professional

With a partner, think about what you have learnt about being professional at work and write a checklist for someone on their first day at work.

B Having an interview

Jamal has a video interview for the Human Resources Assistant (HR Assistant) job at Packaging Solutions Ltd.

Video 3

Watch the video and look at page 86 for more information about a video interview.

1 Before you read

Work with a partner. What do you think you can do wrong at an interview?

2 Reading

13 **Read the beginning of Jamal's video interview with Marie Leblanc, then do the tasks below.**

Marie: Good morning, Mr Ahmed. It's nice to meet you. Can you hear me OK?

Jamal: Good morning, Ms Leblanc. Yes, I can hear and see you. Thank you for inviting me to this interview.

Marie: Well, we always need good trainees in our HR department. Do you mind if I call you Jamal?

Jamal: Of course not. Please do.

Marie: Let me first introduce myself. I'm one of three managers in the HR department. Here on my left is Jane. She looks after the training of new employees. We've read your CV, Jamal – but why don't *you* tell us about yourself and why you want a job in HR.

Jamal: Sorry, I couldn't understand the last thing you said. There was a problem with the connection. Could you repeat the question, please?

Marie: Yes, of course. Why did you decide to apply for a job in HR?

Jamal: Because I enjoy working with people and in teams. I'm not a technical or IT person. In HR you are the link between management and employees. It's about communicating well. I like helping people to solve their problems. And I'm quite good at it.

Marie: What you say about HR is true, but there's also a lot of routine administration and computer work.

Jamal: Of course! I have no problem with that. One of my strengths is that I'm well organized and I don't like it if things aren't neat and tidy.

Marie: I see. Well, your diploma grades are good. You finish high school next month, don't you? Do you mind telling me if you have any other interviews lined up?

Jamal: Yes, I have another interview this week. But I'd like this job because I've already been an intern at Packaging Solutions, and HR, packaging and design really interest me.

A Which statement is correct?

- **a** Ms Leblanc starts by asking questions about Jamal's CV.
- **b** Jamal wants a career in HR because he likes working with people.
- **c** Jamal doesn't want to work with computers.

B Make notes on what Jamal says that makes him a good candidate for the job. Compare your notes with a partner.

EXAMPLE: *Jamal is very polite. For example, he says, "Thank you for inviting me."*

3 Listening

A Listen to more of Jamal's interview. Do you think he will get the job? Why (not)?

14

B Listen again. Fill in the gaps with one or two words.

1 Jamal helped the cook to write short ___
2 If there is an emergency, Jamal can work ___
3 Jamal would like to specialize in health and ___
4 Jamal could start work ___
5 The ___ is not high, but the company is growing and there will be a lot of ___

Interview tips

- Think about body language.
- Always be positive.
- Don't talk too much.
- Listen properly.
- Always tell the truth.

C Which of these expressions did you hear in the interview?

L

Questions
- What are your strengths/weaknesses?
- Can you give me an example of …?
- Where do you see yourself in five years?

Answering questions
- That wouldn't be a problem.
- Could I think about that?

Talking about skills
- I'm an excellent listener.
- I'm good at …
- I'm very motivated.

Describing the job
- We are looking for someone who …
- You would be part of an international team.

G

The *-ing* form of verbs

Um ein Substantiv aus einem Verb zu machen, wird *-ing* hinzugefügt.
- I need train**ing** to do the job.
- Train**ing** helps you do a better job.

Auf einige Verben folgt *-ing* und auf andere folgt der Infinitiv.
- I **enjoy** work**ing** in teams.
- He **wants to find** an apprenticeship.

4 Practice: The *-ing* form

A **Check it out!** Suchen Sie Sätze in dem Dialog auf Seite 28 mit:

1 drei Verben, gefolgt von einem *-ing*
2 drei Verben, gefolgt von einem Infinitiv
3 ein Substantiv, das aus einem Verb mit *-ing* gemacht ist

B Complete the interviewer's questions with the infinitive or the *-ing* form. Look at the verbs you found in the text for help.

1 Why did you decide ___ for this job? (apply)
2 Do you miss ___ in your home country? (live)
3 Do you mind ___ at weekends? (travel)
4 Do you remember ___ those skills? (learn)
5 Where do you plan ___ in five years? (be)
6 When did you learn ___ Spanish? (speak)

☆ ★ Turn to page 95.

C Use the questions from B to make your own short interview dialogue with a partner.

C Learning about different cultures

Mia wants to spend a year abroad. She has found this forum about life in other countries.

1 Reading

15 **Read what the different people said in the forum about small talk, then complete the tasks.**

Small talk around the world

Small talk is part of everyday life in the UK. It may be a conversation with a work colleague or a customer, or a chat between strangers on holiday or in the supermarket. A study has shown that nine out of ten people in the UK have talked about the weather in the last six hours! But what do other cultures think about small talk? Read what some people from around the world said.

Sarah, USA
Like the British, we Americans enjoy small talk. But we're usually more positive about life and don't complain about the weather! We also use phrases like *How are you doing?* or *Have a nice day.*

Björn, Scandinavia
Scandinavians don't think small talk is important. We don't talk about the weather or sport, like you do in the UK. We don't need to fill silences. Small talk is just not part of our culture.

Karen, Germany
It's different in different parts of Germany. Some people don't like 'wasting time' with small talk, but others love a good chat while they are packing their shopping in the supermarket.

Boris, Russia
Russians enjoy discussing events and the news, but we prefer talking in detail about these things. I like talking about the weather, though. Maybe I have some English blood!

Aldo, Brazil
Brazilians love small talk. We are relaxed people, and we will start a conversation with almost anyone. Football is a favourite topic, but only if you know something about it. So be careful if a Brazilian asks you about football.

Sato, China
In China we enjoy chatting about most subjects. A first business meeting is usually for getting to know the other people, not business. We like to hear positive things about China, but avoid politics.

Tariq, India
In India it's polite to talk about general subjects and people's personal lives. Sometimes small talk can get very personal and you may be asked questions you don't want to answer!

A In which countries is small talk not very important?

B Which country do these people come from?

1 We have some of the world's best players.
2 The weather is terrible this week, isn't it?
3 It's 9 o'clock. Let's start the meeting.
4 Do you earn a lot of money?
5 Let's introduce ourselves, then go to lunch.
6 How are you doing?

2 Listening

16 **Listen to five comments (1–5) about the information on the forum. Which headline (a–e) matches each comment?**

a Contact the writer
b Training in small talk
c Culture much more important
d Prefers a quiet life
e Small talk better than arguments

☆ ★ **Turn to page 95.**

3 Words, words, words: Keeping a conversation going

Mia has an interview at a British company. She is talking to Sandy, another candidate, while she is waiting.

L

Showing an interest	Showing understanding	Showing surprise
I get it.	Tell me more.	Seriously?
That's very true.	And then what?	Are you joking?
I don't follow (you).	Go ahead.	I never guessed.
I can imagine how you felt.	Well done!	What a … !
I'm sorry to hear that.	That's amazing/incredible!	That's a … .
I know what you mean.	That reminds me of …	How … .

A Mia needs help to keep the conversation going. What does she want to say? Use expressions from the box.

Sandy:	Mia:
1 India is an amazing place.	*Erzähl weiter.* EXAMPLE: Tell me more.
2 Shall I tell you about my trip to India?	*Nur zu.*
3 First I spent five days in Mumbai.	*Das ist ja toll!*
4 There's a festival where you throw colours at each other.	*Ich verstehe nicht.*
5 It's the festival of colour. Everyone throws coloured powder.	*Und was danach?*
6 They go to each other's houses, wash and change their clothes.	*Wie interessant.*

B What would you say? Use an expression from the box and ask a question.

1 They offered me the job! I never expected it in a million years.
EXAMPLE: That's incredible! When do you start?
2 The interview didn't go well. I was so nervous.
3 Do you understand? I can't tell you any more at the moment.
4 With my new e-bike I get to work in half the time.
5 Then the customer suddenly started shouting at me.

4 Pairwork: A role play

Speed chat You are waiting with another person for an interview. Talk to the other person (your partner) for a few minutes before the HR assistant collects you. Look at this list and decide if you should or shouldn't talk about the things.

- the weather
- the company
- other interviews you have had
- holidays
- sport
- how good you are for the job
- your journey to the interview
- food

Skills practice: Preparing meetings

Regelmäßige Treffen und Besprechungen zwischen Mitarbeitern oder externen Partnern sind ein wichtiger Teil des Arbeitslebens. Wie aber ist die Vorbereitung und wie läuft eine Besprechung ab?

Get it right: *Schritte zu einer erfolgreichen Besprechung*

- Legen Sie einen Termin für die Besprechung fest: Tag, Uhrzeit, Dauer.
- Buchen Sie *(book)* einen Besprechungsraum *(meeting room)* und sorgen Sie für Getränke und die notwendige Ausstattung *(projector, laptop, etc.)*.
- Schicken Sie die Einladungen.
- Senden Sie zeitnah zur Besprechung allen Teilnehmenden die Tagesordnung *(agenda)* zu.
- Eine Besprechung hat in der Regel folgenden Ablauf: Der/Die Gesprächsleiter/in *(chairperson)* begrüßt alle und geht zu den Tagesordnungspunkten über.

A Finding a suitable date and meeting room

Jamal now works for Packaging Solutions Ltd. He is helping to organize a meeting. He has to find a date and time that suits everyone and then book a meeting room.

a) Look at the participants' calendars. When have they all got time for the meeting?
Partner A: Look at the calendars of the three participants here.
Partner B: Go to file 6 on page 91.

Paola	Marie	Ryan
Mon:	Mon:	Mon: meeting a.m.
Tues: meeting p.m.	Tues: meeting p.m.	Tues: meeting p.m.
Wed:	Wed: meeting p.m.	Wed: meeting a.m.
Thurs: meeting a.m.	Thurs: meeting p.m.	Thurs: meeting p.m.
Fri: holiday	Fri: meeting p.m.	Fri:

EXAMPLE:

A: Is Elena busy on Monday morning?

B: Yes, she is. What about Paola? Is she busy then?

b) Now Jamal needs a meeting room that is big enough for the 6 participants (but not too big) and is free. Look at the list of meeting rooms and decide which two would work best with the date you found in a). (x = booked)

Room details	Mon	Tues	Wed	Thur	Fri
Room 600 (max. 4)		x	x	x	x
Room 450 (max. 10)	x	x			x
Room 101 (max. 20)	x		x	x	x
Room 005 (max. 6)					
Room 207 (max. 50)		x		x	
Room 603 (max. 10)			x	x	

B Listening

17 **Jane and Jamal discuss the agenda for the meeting. Jamal makes notes. Listen to the dialogue and find the mistakes Jamal has made. Rewrite the agenda so it is correct.**

Meeting agenda

Date: Mon, Jan 13 **Time:** 1:30 p.m. **Room:** 603

1:30 p.m.	Introduction by Marie Leblanc
1:45 p.m.	Stefan Braun: language course programme suggestions
2:30 p.m.	COFFEE
3:00 p.m.	Group work: discussion of Stefan's suggestions
4:15 p.m.	COFFEE
4:30 p.m.	Group feedback and discussion
5:10 p.m.	Conclusions (Stefan)
	Other business (Marie)
6:00 p.m.	End of meeting

Einige Länder, z.B. UK, USA, Kanada und Australien, geben die Uhrzeit mit *a.m.* (0 bis 11:59 Uhr) und *p.m.* (12 bis 23:59 Uhr) an.

Listen again. List three more things Jamal has to do before the meeting.

C Mediation

Stefan Braun, der an der Besprechung teilnimmt, hat bereits einige Sprachkurse in Firmen gehalten. Jamal soll aus diesem Text von Stefans Website eine Zusammenfassung schreiben und an die Teilnehmer der Besprechung, zusammen mit der Tagesordnung, schicken. Helfen Sie Jamal mit seinem Text. Sie können ein Wörterbuch verwenden.

Stefans Sprachkurse

Ich heiße Stefan Braun, komme ursprünglich aus Süddeutschland und wohne seit 15 Jahren mit meiner Familie in England. Ich arbeite gerne mit Firmen zusammen, um Ihre Mitarbeiter in der deutschen Sprache zu schulen und ihnen zu helfen, sich in deutschen Firmen zurechtzufinden. Ich habe 15 Jahre in verschiedenen deutschen Firmen gearbeitet und schon einiges an Kenntnissen gesammelt, die ich gerne weitergebe.

Zusätzlich finde ich es wichtig, dass die Mitarbeiter wissen, wie deutsche Firmen funktionieren und was anders als in englischen Firmen ist, Mitarbeiter fangen z.B. morgens um ca. 7 Uhr an, die Kleiderordnung am Arbeitsplatz ist weniger formell als in englischen Firmen, Vorgesetzte werden mit *Herr* oder *Frau* statt mit Vornamen angesprochen, die Mittagspause beginnt oft bereits um ca. 11:45 Uhr.

Darüber hinaus werden allgemeine Informationen über Deutschland vermittelt, welche gut zu wissen sind, wenn man dort geschäftlich oder privat unterwegs ist: Die Läden haben z.B. sonntags geschlossen, im Restaurant erhält die Bedienung immer Trinkgeld, bei Reisen mit der Bahn lässt man Fahrgäste erst aussteigen, bevor man einsteigt, wenn man es eilig hat, läuft man links die Rolltreppe hinauf.

Project page: Dos and don'ts

You now know more about professional life. Work in a group and make a short dos and don'ts video.

A Divide the class into three groups. Each group has a different topic.

Topics for video:
At an interview
In the office
Meeting people for the first time

B Half of the group makes a list of the dos for your topic and the other half makes a list of the don'ts.

C Compare your lists and decide which three of each are the most important. How can you act them out? Decide together.

D Decide who will take on each role.

Scriptwriter:	Writes what everyone says and does.
Director:	Tells everyone what to do while filming.
Camera operator:	Operates the camera.
Actors:	Appear and speak in the video.

Working together

L

Deciding roles
- I'd like to be responsible for …
- Paul is good at … .
- He should be the … .
- Would you like to … ?

Asking for / Offering help
- Can you help me with … ?
- Would you like some help with … ?

Deciding together
- Do we all agree that … ?
- I (don't) think that …

E Make your video.

F Show your videos in class. Give each other feedback. Look at page 100 for some useful feedback phrases.

Snapshot

What was your favourite thing in this unit?

What important thing did you learn?

What do you need to work on?

Starting your career 4

Warm-up: Workplaces

A Find the workplace for each of the jobs.

Job	Workplace
carpenter ■ nurse car mechanic ■ receptionist flight attendant ■ immigration officer customer service agent medical technician nursery assistant ■ shop assistant	airport ■ call centre department store hospital ■ hotel nursery school laboratory ■ plane workshop ■ garage

B Work with a partner. Match each picture (1–6) to one of the jobs in A. Find pictures on the internet for the other jobs.

1 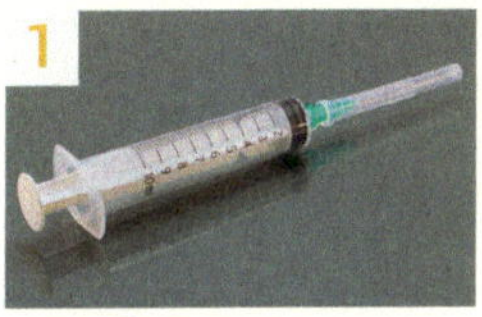

syringe

2 

stamp

3 

key card

4 

saw

5 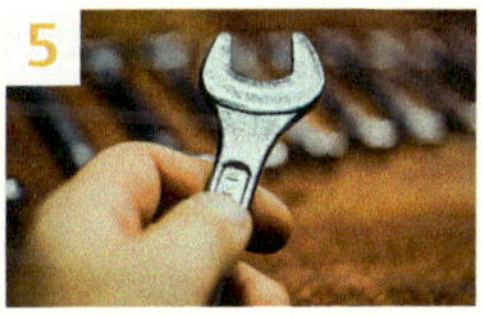

spanner

6 

uniform

C Look at the list of things employees say are important in an ideal workplace. What is important for you? Rank the things 1 (most important) – 6 (not so important).

- Good salary
- Benefits – workplace gym, free travel to work, bonuses
- Friendly, helpful colleagues
- Flexible working hours
- Company training programme
- Canteen – reduced price meals

D In class talk about your list from C and give your reasons for your choices.

EXAMPLE:

I think the most important thing is ... because ...

4 Starting your career

A Showing a new employee around

It's Tracy's first day as an IT support trainee at Vegan Snacks Ltd. Rahul, another trainee, meets her.

1 Before you read

Tomorrow is your first day in a new job. What will you have to do? Discuss with a partner.

2 Reading

> **!**
> employer – employee
> trainer – trainee

Read the dialogue, then complete the tasks below.

18

Rahul: Hello, Tracy Black? My name's Rahul. I'm a trainee at Vegan Snacks Ltd. Anna Rossi, our IT team leader, asked me to show you around.

Tracy: Good morning, Rahul. Thank you for coming. I feel a bit nervous.

Rahul: That's normal. I've been here for a year and I still remember my first day. But don't worry. It's all pretty informal here. The plan is that first I show you your desk, then we'll walk through the factory and the offices and I'll explain things as we go. After that, I'll take you to Anna's office as she would like to welcome you. After she has spoken to you, I'll leave you to check out your desk, and at 12:30 there's lunch with the team. You'll meet …

Mr Ash: Good morning, Rahul. And you must be the new IT trainee. I can't stop, I'm late for a meeting. We'll talk later. Best of luck.

Tracy: Nice to meet you.

Rahul: That was Mr Ash, Sales Manager. He's always in a rush. I've never seen him have a long conversation with anybody! I've got a floor plan here, so before we start the tour let's sit down and I'll explain it to you. We're here at the entrance. The factory, where they produce the tasty vegan snacks, is at the back of this building. Next to the factory is Product Development, where they develop the recipes. Maybe they'll let us test some.

Tracy: Do they let meat eaters in?

Rahul: Ha ha. I think all meat eaters have come out alive so far! At the end of the factory is Packing and Shipping. The lorries load and unload their goods here. This is the office building; it has three floors. The ground floor is Sales and Marketing, and the first floor is Accounts and Management. IT Support, that's us, is up on the second floor, together with HR. We have a great view! Oh, look at the time … there's only an hour before your meeting with Anna. The lift is down the corridor on the left. Ah, that's Jenny Mills coming to speak to us. Be nice to her. She's always complaining about the computer network.

Tracy: I'm all smiles!

Rahul: Hi Jenny. I'd like to introduce …

A Rahul has planned his and Tracy's morning. Put his notes (a–f) in the right order.

a factory/office visit
b lunch with the team
c take Tracy to meet Anna
d show Tracy her desk
e leave Tracy alone
f meet Tracy

B Look at the floor plan of Vegan Snack Ltd. What are the names of the departments (a–f)?

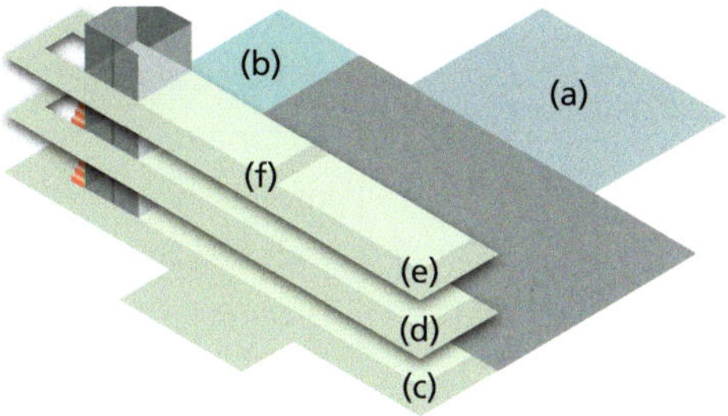

> **!**
> Erdgeschoss:
> ground floor BE
> first floor AE

G

Das ***simple past*** wird verwendet, wenn man ausdrücken will, dass etwas zu einem bestimmten Zeitpunkt in der Vergangenheit geschehen ist. **Signalwörter:** *yesterday, last … (Monday, week), in … (2019), … (a week) ago*	Das ***present perfect*** wird verwendet, wenn man sagen will, dass etwas geschehen ist oder man drückt damit aus, seit wann oder wie lange ein Zustand schon andauert. **Signalwörter:** *just, already, ever, never, (not) yet, lately, recently, for, since*

*I **met** the team in the morning. But I **didn't meet** Niki. I **have just met** her in the cafeteria.*
*I **had** a car accident an hour ago. I**'ve crashed** my mum's new car.*

3 Practice: Simple past or present perfect?

A Check it out! **Finden Sie zwei Beispiele von *simple past* und zwei Beispiele von *present perfect* im Text auf Seite 36.**

B Read Tracy's list of jobs for her first week. It's Wednesday morning. What did she do on Monday and Tuesday and what hasn't she done yet?

1 Read history of Vegan Snacks *(Friday)*
Tracy hasn't read the history of Vegan Snacks yet.
2 Sign contract in HR *(Monday)*
3 Test the Alpha software *(Friday)*
4 Open a company email account *(Monday)*
5 Install the network update *(Wednesday)*
6 Pick up door entry card *(Monday)*
7 Read and sign the security rules *(Tuesday)*

☆ ★ **Turn to page 95.**

4 Pairwork: Giving directions

Student A is visiting Vegan Snacks Ltd. and finds a place on the floor plan above. Student A asks Student B, who is working at reception, for directions. Did you find the place? Now swap roles.

EXAMPLE:

> Can you tell me where the ... is?

> Let me see. It's straight ahead and next to the ...

> **L**
> **Giving directions**
>
> It's on the ground/first/top floor.
> It's opposite / in front of / behind / near the …
> It's straight ahead / on the left / on the right.
> Turn left/right at the …
> It's the first/second on the left/right.

B Passing your trial period

Mia has a job as a nursery assistant at an international nursery school. She has also been working at the refugee centre during her trial period.

Video 4

Watch the video and look at page 86 for more information about your first day in a new job.

1 Before you listen

Work with a partner. Think of reasons why some new employees may not pass their trial period.

EXAMPLE:

Some people make too many private phone calls.

Yes, I agree. Another reason could be that they make mistakes ...

L

Phrases with *make*

make sense – *Sinn ergeben*
make a difference – *etw bewirken*
make time – *Zeit finden*

2 Listening

19 **A Match the English words and expressions with the German ones.**

1	trial period	**a**	Erklärung
2	permanent contract	**b**	machen, was am besten ist
3	short of volunteers	**c**	Probezeit
4	teamwork	**d**	zu wenige Freiwillige
5	explanation	**e**	Teamarbeit
6	do what is best	**f**	unbefristeter Arbeitsvertrag

B Mia is talking to Lisa, her boss at the nursery school, about her trial period. Listen and complete the sentences with the correct answer (a, b or c).

1 Lisa wants to speak to Mia because her trial period …
   a has ended.
   b finishes in two months.
   c is not going well.

2 Mia explains she …
   a has problems with the team.
   b is busy at the refugee centre.
   c has problems with her parents.

3 At the end of the conversation Mia agrees to …
   a think about her future.
   b be a better teacher.
   c change how she works.

C Listen again and make notes in German explaining:

1 Warum ist der Kindergarten mit Mias Arbeit nicht zufrieden?
2 Was macht Mia im Flüchtlingsheim, dass sie so müde ist?
3 Welche Entscheidung muss Mia treffen? Warum fällt es ihr schwer, sie zu treffen?

G

***If*-sentences Type 1 …**

verwendet man, wenn man sagen möchte, was unter bestimmten Bedingungen passiert. Bedingungssätze bestehen aus einem Hauptsatz und einem Nebensatz mit *if*. Typ 1 drückt Bedingungen aus, die leicht erfüllt werden können. Die Folge dieser Bedingung ist wahrscheinlich.

If-Satz: simple present	Hauptsatz: *will*-Futur
*If Mia **stays** at the nursery school,*	*she **will become** a good teacher.*
*If people **stop** helping refugees,*	*they **won't learn** German.*

! Verwenden Sie nie *will* im *if*-Teil:
If you ~~will~~ want to discuss it, I'll call you.

3 Practice: *If*-sentences Type 1

A **Check it out!** **Hören Sie Mias Gespräch noch einmal. Hören Sie die drei *if*-Sätze?**

B **Complete the *if*-sentences with the correct form of the verbs in brackets.**

1. If you *dress* smartly, people *will know* that you are serious about your job. (dress, know)
2. If you often ___, your colleagues ___ you are friendly. (smile, think)
3. If you always ___ on time for meetings, you ___ a good impression. (arrive, make)
4. If you ___ carefully to your manager, you ___ a lot. (listen, learn)
5. If you ___ a busy colleague, people ___ you. (help, notice)
6. If you ___ computer games at work, you ___ your trial period. (play, not pass)

☆ ★ **Turn to page 96.**

4 Discussion

Over the weekend Mia found Mike's post on a careers advice website.

@mike314: It's week three of my first permanent job since leaving college. If this is the right job for me, things will have to change. At the interview, they told me that there was a lot of contact with people in the job: meetings, discussions, etc. I really need contact with others. Since I started, I have sat at my computer all day, with just a few minutes for small talk with colleagues. It doesn't seem things will change soon, because today they gave me my first proper project. It will take months, and the only communication with others will be through emails. If I quit, I will have to do so in my trial period. It wouldn't look good on my CV though.

A **Work with a partner. What advice would you give Mike? Think about these points:**

- Life worse with a full-time job?
- Talk to someone at work?
- Quit now or see if things get better?
- Next job better?

EXAMPLE:

> If Mike quits, he might not get another job.

> I don't agree. There are ...

B **Talk about the main points of your discussion in class.**

C Working days around the world

Young Careers, a website for jobseekers, asked young people about their everyday lives at work.

1 Reading

A Get into small groups. Each person chooses a different text.

20

1 Read your text and make notes. You have three minutes.

2 Now close your books. Tell your partners what you know about Jill, Angus or Jack.

Jill, a home care nurse in Alberta, Canada

Today I had the early shift at our small hospital, where I helped deliver a baby. After that it was non-stop all morning. I helped a patient who is learning to walk again, I checked that a man had a warm house to go home to and I listened to a mother whose son has just had a bad car accident. In the afternoon I had four visits with quite a long drive between them. I gave a man with diabetes a complete check-up and stayed with him after my shift had ended. Every day is different in my job. You never know who will come through the door. People of all ages, with different problems; some of them are even friends or neighbours. You need to be caring, independent and skilled because you are often alone.

Angus, a customer service agent from Inverness, Scotland

7:30 a.m.: Meditating or exercise help me start the day and are helpful when you work from home.
9 a.m.: Coffee at my desk, I log into the system and greet the team. If they don't need me, I'll read my emails.
9:30 a.m.: I start taking calls from customers. I have about 15 calls a day. People in different situations need different types of insurance. But I also make time to load the dishwasher or do my laundry!
1 p.m.: Lunch. I try not to eat at my desk. (It doesn't always work!)
2 p.m.: Back to work. More calls or follow-ups from the morning.
4 p.m.: I take a break. It's easy to forget breaks, and suddenly you haven't moved for six hours!
6 p.m.: I turn off my laptop and try not to look at work stuff. It feels good to help customers.

Jack, a marine electrician in Queensland, Australia

After my apprenticeship in Brisbane, I got a job as a marine electrician. Boats have always interested me. It's specialized work, so I'm always learning on the job. There's lots of electrics and electronics on boats: navigation systems, solar panels, wind generators - even the toilet systems. We start work early and finish late. Customers bring their boats to the boatyard or we work on them in the water. Today a guy came with a new boat that had no lights that worked. We found the problem and repaired it. I also pick up the spare parts we need from the warehouse. Today I collected a watermaker for a luxury yacht. We'll install it tomorrow! I really enjoy my job. Everybody is relaxed and loves boats.

B Read the texts on page 40 again. Find the following in the texts.

1. One job Jill did in the morning and one job she did in the afternoon.
2. The things Angus tries to do before work, at lunch and after work.
3. Two things Jack did today.

C Decide whether these statements are true or false. Correct the false statements.

1. Jill's patients lived close together.
   False, she had quite a long drive.
2. In Jill's job it is difficult to plan the day.
3. Angus talks to colleagues before he answers calls.
4. Angus works six hours before he has a break.
5. Jack has no qualifications.
6. Jack only works in the boatyard.
7. Jack will install a battery on a yacht tomorrow.

2 Words, words, words: Nurse, office worker, electrician

Complete the sentences. All the words you need are in the texts on page 40.

1. Nurses in the hospital do three ___. Jill doesn't like to work nights.
2. Sometimes doctors have to ___ babies at night.
3. In the morning I need my password to ___.
4. When we have an online meeting, we always ___ each other before we look at the agenda.
5. Jack can't repair the old boat if he doesn't have the ___.
6. All the goods go to a large ___ first, then they go to shops or private customers.

☆ ★ **Turn to page 96.**

3 Mediation

Read this article about casual Friday from the Young Careers website.

Casual Friday

Friday is the end of the working week, when most office workers look forward to the weekend. Many businesses in western countries have 'casual Friday', where staff dress informally and wear comfortable clothes. What should you wear on casual Friday? It is important to dress relaxed but stay professional. If you have a meeting with a customer, it is better to skip casual Friday. If you are new in a company and not sure what is acceptable, it is best to ask your boss for some guidelines. These might help you though:

Shorts are not appropriate for work. Keep them for the weekends.
Jeans may be acceptable, but they are better with a more formal shirt or blouse.
Flip-flops don't belong in the office.
Stains on your clothes look bad. Only wear clean clothes to the office.
T-shirts with messages or symbols are risky. Choose plain colours.
Tight clothes, short skirts: You don't need to show off your muscles or your figure at work. Gym clothing is also not appropriate. Remember you're at work, not on holiday.

Ihr/e Freund/in ist auf Arbeitsuche und er/sie weiß nicht, was ‚casual Friday' ist. Schreiben Sie einen zusammenhängenden Text auf Deutsch in ganzen Sätzen. Erklären Sie, was 'casual Friday' ist, was bei den Überlegungen, wie man sich anzieht, hilfreich sein könnte und worauf man bei der Auswahl der Kleidung achten sollte.

Skills practice: Giving a short presentation

Es kommt im Berufsleben manchmal vor, dass man eine kurze Präsentation vor einer Gruppe von Kollegen oder vor Kunden halten muss. Bei ‚Giving a short presentation' geht es darum, etwas mit einem bestimmten Schwerpunkt oder ein bestimmtes Thema kurz vorzustellen.

Get it right: *Wie bereite ich eine kurze Präsentation vor?*

- Recherchieren Sie den Inhalt Ihrer Präsentation und planen Sie den Ablauf.
- Lesen Sie während der Präsentation nicht von Ihren Notizen ab, sondern schauen Sie Ihr Publikum an.
- Sagen Sie zu Beginn, wie Ihre Präsentation strukturiert ist *(My talk has three parts …)*, damit die Zuhörer besser folgen können.
- Beenden Sie Ihre Präsentation mit einer Zusammenfassung der wichtigsten Punkte oder einem Schlusswort.
- Vergessen Sie nicht, auf Ihre Körpersprache und Ihr Aussehen zu achten. Stehen Sie aufrecht und suchen Sie den Augenkontakt zu den Zuhörern. Dadurch wirken Sie professionell und werden ernst genommen.

A Welcoming visitors

21 **Jamal has to give a short presentation to some visitors. Listen to his presentation and complete the text.**

Good afternoon. **(1)** *Welcome to* Packaging Solutions Ltd. My name is Jamal Ahmed, I'm an assistant in the HR department. **(2)**, I'd like to tell you something about the company, **(3)** I'll give you a short tour of the plant and **(4)** I'll take you to Marie Leblanc's office for your meeting. Packaging Solutions Ltd. started here in Toronto in 2014, but it **(5)** and we now have production plants in four countries, including the USA and Germany. **(6)**, we make high-quality packaging for medicines. **(7)**, our biggest customers are pharmaceutical companies. We have more than 500 employees and sales of C$65 million. That's all the facts for now. **(8)**, I'll tell you more as we go around. If you have any questions, **(9)**.

B Useful phrases

a) Decide if the phrases would be used at the beginning or the end of a presentation.

1 Welcome to …
2 That completes my presentation.
3 The topic I'll talk about first is …
4 My presentation has looked at …
5 Thank you for listening.
6 I'd like to start by …

b) Choose the correct connecting words.

1 Jamal is very friendly, although/so they often ask him to meet visitors.
2 He has to stop what he is doing, but/if the people he meets are often interesting.
3 First,/So, he greets the group, then he introduces himself.
4 He doesn't often take visitors around the plant so that/because most have been before.
5 Visitors often have questions. Finally,/For example, they ask about recycling packaging.

C Important information

There is an open day at your school for new students and their parents. When they arrive you have one minute to give them three pieces of important information (in German). With a partner decide on the important information you think they need to know. Tell the class your pieces of information.

D Typical mistakes

22 **a) Listen to the extracts from five bad presentations.**

1 Which speaker did not look up important English phrases before the presentation?
That was speaker ...
2 Which speaker did not take the presentation seriously?
3 Which speaker is unprepared and disorganized?
4 Which speaker does not have a structured presentation?
5 Which speaker sounds bored and doesn't want to give the presentation?

b) Can you think of any other mistakes people make when they give a presentation? Make a list with a partner.

E Give a presentation

Work in a small group. Each person prepares a one-minute presentation about a topic in the word cloud (or their own topic).

my summer job
my career plans
home office
my part-time job
clothes for work
social media
a country I'd like to work in
holidays I enjoy
my workplace
how I relax
how to do something

L

Hello, my name is … I'd like to talk about …	A good example is …
Firstly, …, then … and finally …	Does anyone have any questions?
My next point is …	Thanks.

F Your checklist

With a partner think about the things you need to remember when you prepare a presentation and when you give a presentation. Write a checklist. Compare your checklist with another pair in the class. Are they the same? Did you forget anything? You can use your checklist for your next school presentation and add anything that might be missing from it. There is always room on a checklist for new things.

EXAMPLE:

Remember to speak clearly and structure the presentation well.

Make sure you summarize your points at the end.

Project page: Finding out about an unusual job

You are going to present some information about an unusual job.

A Read the information about these jobs. Think about the people's workplace, their tools and their typical day.

White hacker
Hackers are not all bad. Computer programmers can use their skills for white hacking. Companies employ them to check their networks so that the bad guys can't get in.

Personal shopper
Do you want to spend somebody else's money? Some rich people are too busy to do their own shopping. They employ personal shoppers to do it for them.

Chocolate maker
Would you like to work with chocolate all day? Yes? A chocolate maker is a professional chef who specializes in making amazing chocolates.

EXAMPLE:

> I think that the white hacker works in a home office.

> Right, and I expect he/she sits at a computer all day.

B Work in small groups. In your group choose a job from A. Think of some useful words connected to the job and use the internet to find out more information about the job. Make notes.

C Prepare a presentation about the unusual job – but don't say the name of the job. Each person in your group presents for one minute.

D The rest of the class tries to guess which job you have presented.

E Give each other feedback on your presentations. Look at page 100 for some useful feedback phrases.

Snapshot

What was your favourite thing in this unit?

What important thing did you learn?

What do you need to work on?

Just a trend? 5

Warm-up: Friendlier alternatives

A **Describe the pictures on the right. What is the problem? Can you do anything to stop these problems?**

B **Plastic isn't good for the environment, but there are lots of alternatives. Match these environmentally friendly materials with the photos (A–F).**

flour ▪ soap ▪ metal ▪ coconut ▪ wood ▪ recycled paper

C **Speed chat:** **What plastic products do you use every day?**

EXAMPLE

My coffee to-go cup is made of paper, but the top is made of plastic.

That's true. Do we need the lid? The stick for stirring my coffee is also plastic. What else is plastic?

D **Do a class survey. What things do you use that there is an environmentally friendly alternative for? How often do you use it?**

	sometimes	often	never
shampoo	III	II	I
fast fashion (T-shirts, trainers)	…		
make-up			
meat			
…			

5 Just a trend?

A Improving the company image

At Vegan Snacks they want to ban single-use plastics. Mr A, the Sales Manager, starts a discussion in an online forum.

Video 5

Watch the video and look at page 87 for more information about alternatives to plastic.

1 Before you read

Have you ever looked at an online forum for an answer to a question? Was the answer helpful? Did you write a comment too and get a reply?

2 Reading

23 **A Read the discussion on the online forum about plastic, then answer the questions below.**

? Mr A	We are a small vegan food production company. If we banned single-use plastics, it would be good for our image. Staff would feel they work for an eco-friendly company that cares about its impact on the environment. Some people are still against the idea, so we haven't taken a final decision yet. If we went ahead, we would begin by reducing plastic in our offices.
Go31	That's a great plan! If I were you, in the cafeteria or shop if you have one, I would only sell water in glass bottles. Put water coolers in all the offices with filtered tap water and no plastic cups. And you must ban plastic straws!
Barry1234	The knives and forks in the cafeteria should be metal, and for takeaway meals wooden. Give all staff a reusable plastic-free coffee cup for the coffee machine. If the machine uses coffee capsules, you will need to check if they are reusable.
Go31	If you started your 'no plastic' project with a talk and film about plastic pollution in the ocean, perhaps the unhappy people would be motivated to change their habits.
Sania	Don't forget to ask the employees what they think. They often have some of the most creative solutions. Why not invite them to brainstorming meetings? If I worked for your company, I would plan a meeting in each department so that everyone had the chance to speak.
Green+++	Talk to your office suppliers. Persuade them to use more reusable packaging. This would also save you money on your waste collections. I've found that caring for the environment doesn't have to be more expensive.
Sania	If you can, at the end of the first six months calculate the amount of plastic you have saved. Share your success with customers, suppliers and employees. It's good for your reputation, and they may follow your example. We went through this process last year. We now don't buy or sell any single-use plastic. Good luck Mr A!

1 Why has Vegan Snacks not made a decision yet?
2 A ban would improve Vegan Snack's what?
3 How could employees help?

B Copy this table and write down the suggestions made in the online forum on page 46.

Name	Suggestions
Go31	*Sell water in glass bottles.*
Barry1234	*Use ...*
Sania	
Green+++	

Plastic facts

	Per year	Years in ocean	Recycled
Bottles	500 billion	450	14%
Bags	1 trillion	up to 1,000	1 in 7

C Class brainstorm. Think of some ideas to reduce the use of plastic in your school.

EXAMPLE: If ..., then we would reduce the use of plastic.

G

***If*-sentences Type 2 ...**

drücken Bedingungen aus, die weniger wahrscheinlich sind. Die Folge dieser Bedingung ist ungewiss.
Bedingungssätze beginnen mit dem *if*-Teil oder dem Hauptsatz. Nach dem *if*-Teil kommt immer ein Komma.

If-Satz: simple past Hauptsatz: *would* + Infinitiv
*If we **used** fewer takeaway cups, then we **would** reduce the use of plastic.*

3 Practice: *If*-sentences Type 2

A Check it out! Suchen Sie im Text auf Seite 46 alle Sätze, die mit ‚*If* ...' anfangen und schreiben Sie sie auf. Schauen Sie sie an und finden Sie heraus, was die Bedingungen und Folgen sind. Wann verwenden Sie *If-Sätze Typ 2*?

EXAMPLE: **If we banned single-use plastics, it would be good for our image.**
Bedingung: Einwegplastik verbieten Folge: das eigene Image verbessern

B Mr A liked Sania's suggestion in the forum and held a brainstorming meeting. Look at what the factory workers said and finish their sentences.

1 If we used plastic for 3D printing, we would ...
2 If Hassan came to the next meeting, he would ...
3 If we did that, our products ...
4 If we sorted the plastic into different colours, it ...
5 If we made a list of the plastic we use, we ...
6 If we looked for another type of packaging, I'm sure we ...

☆ **Turn to page 96.**

4 What about you?

A Think about the things you can change in your life so that you use fewer plastic products. Write four sentences with your ideas.

EXAMPLE: *If I bought a bamboo coffee to-go cup, I wouldn't need one from the bakery.*

B Talk about your ideas in class.

B Green marketing

Tracy is interested in sales and marketing. She is doing an online course in her spare time.

1 Before you read

Look at these symbols for environmental products. Explain what they mean.

1 FAIRTRADE 2 FSC 3 FORESTS FOR ALL FOREVER 4 BLAUER ENGEL DAS UMWELTZEICHEN 5 GLOBAL ORGANIC TEXTILE STANDARD · GOTS ·

2 Mediation

24 **Read the introduction to a module in Tracy's course, then complete the task below.**

Module 3.1 Marketing a green business

Consumers are interested in buying green products, but they are suspicious of 'greenwashing' or marketing techniques which present a false eco-friendly image. What should genuinely eco-friendly companies do to advertise their products?

In this module we will look at the following marketing strategies:

- The business as a whole. Make it 100% eco-friendly. If you sell organic food, for example, will your customers accept traditional plastic packaging?
- Make sure the staff know that you are an eco-friendly business. Where do the materials come from, and can the staff answer questions about them? Always try to use local suppliers.
- Tell customers what the business is doing for the environment. Highlight your successes and explain where more work is being done. The company website is ideal for this.
- Apply for an environmental label as an eco-friendly company in the industry. This will show that experts have checked everything.
- Invest in digital marketing to reduce the use of paper. This will also save money. Remember an image can get people's attention and a picture is worth a thousand words.
- Make the eco-friendly changes the company is carrying out into a story. Use photos, films and statements from the people who have seen the changes. An audience connects to a story and remembers it later.

Ihr/e Freund/in, der/die sehr umweltbewusst lebt, arbeitet in einem traditionsreichen Unternehmen. Sie wissen, dass er/sie die Firma überzeugen möchte, mehr für die Umwelt zu tun, und deshalb Interesse an diesem Text hätte.

Schreiben Sie einen zusammenhängenden Text auf Deutsch in ganzen Sätzen. Erwähnen Sie folgende Punkte aus dem Text:

Was denken Konsumenten über nachhaltige Produkte? ▪ Worüber sollte man alle informieren? ▪ Wie hilft einer Firma ein Umweltzeichen? ▪ Was ist der Vorteil von digitalem Marketing? ▪ Wie können Geschichten einer Firma helfen, sich positiv zu zeigen?

3 Words, words, words: Marketing and the consumer

Look at the text on page 48 and find the English for these German words.

1 misstrauisch
2 Image
3 echt
4 als Ganzes
5 Mitarbeiter
6 hervorheben
7 Kennzeichnung
8 Aufmerksamkeit
9 Aussagen

4 Listening

25 **A Listen to the interview between Tracy's course teacher and Liv Huston about bamboo sunglasses. Which is the best heading for the interview?**

a Why plastic sunglasses are bad news
b Sales campaign for a green product
c How to sell new sunglasses
d Consumer feelings about green products

B Listen to the interview again and complete Tracy's notes.

1 Marketing eco-friendly products is different

- (1) want to support eco-friendly products.
- But (2) do you find them?

2 Steps in the campaign

Liv's job was to convince customers to (3). How?

- Only (4) of plastic sunglasses are (5). She gave customers the facts and asked, "What happens if you (6) our glasses?"
- To show that the company is serious about the (7), we promised:
  ... to support Save Our Oceans and (8) of profits.
  ... to clean 10 kilos of plastic (9) for every 10 pairs of glasses sold.

3 Results

- High sales
- (10) were new customers

☆ **Turn to page 97.**

5 Talking about an advert

A Work with a partner. Look at the advert on the right and answer the questions.
What can you see in the advert?
What is the advert about?
How do you know?

B Find an environmental advert on the internet. Show your class and tell them about it. Describe the advert and explain what it is for. Then tell the class what you think of the advert.

C Protecting our environment

After talking to Tracy, Mia wants to talk to a political youth group she belongs to about the environment and how to save energy.

1 Reading

26 **Mia found these tips to help her with her talk. Read the tips and look at the pictures of things you should not do for the environment. Then complete the tasks below.**

A Only go by car when it's necessary. Walk or cycle. It's better for your health, saves money and reduces dangerous greenhouse gases which are responsible for climate change.

B Save clean water. We should only use 1% of the earth's water. Don't stay in the shower for more than 5 minutes. Use a glass of water when you brush your teeth.

C Modern appliances are much more energy efficient than ten years ago. Buy a new washing machine or fridge with an energy label A. It's worth the price in the long run.

D Don't waste food. Our landfills are full of leftover food where it turns into greenhouse gas. Don't buy more than you need. Have fun using leftover food in new recipes. Remember the 'sell-by' date on the packet is when the shop must sell it by, not the date when you have to eat the food.

E Reduce the amount of packaging you bring home. Buy food 'loose', without packaging, and take your own containers to shops. Takeaway food containers are a problem, so take your own container when you get a takeaway. Take your own coffee cup when you go to your favourite café!

F Try not to buy food which has travelled by air so that it stays fresh. Air transport uses a lot of energy and produces greenhouse gases. It's best to buy fresh fruit and vegetables that are grown in your local area when they are in season.

G Buy LED lights. They are more expensive but they use 90% less energy and last much longer than traditional light bulbs. They are also 100% recyclable.

H Don't throw away your fruit juice bottles and jam jars. You can re-use them. They are free containers, or you can just use them for your plants or flowers.

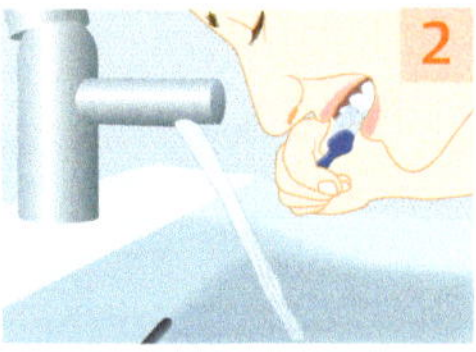

1 Match the tips (A–H) with the pictures (1–8).

2 Use the tips to say what is wrong in each picture.

EXAMPLE: *In picture 6 there are cars in a traffic jam. But tip ... says you should ...*

2 Words, words, words: The environment

Complete the text with the English for the German words in the box. There are three more words than you need. All the words are in the text on page 50.

Behälter ▪ energieeffizient ▪ Essensreste ▪ Erde ▪ Haltbarkeitsdatum ▪ Haushaltsgeräte
Klimawandel ▪ langfristig ▪ Mülldeponien ▪ wiederverwertbar ▪ Treibhausgas

In the 21st century, **(1)** has made the **(2)** much warmer. The **(3)** which comes from **(4)** is part of the problem. These are full of our waste which is not **(5)**.
What can we do to take better care of the environment? There are small things. We can, for example, buy electrical **(6)** which are **(7)** with an energy label A. And when we go shopping or get a takeaway, we can take our own **(8)**.

☆ **Turn to page 97.**

3 How eco-friendly are you?

A **Work with a partner. Do the quiz and find out how green you are.**

Partner A: **Answer questions 1–8 below yourself, then answer partner B's questions 9–16. Now ask partner B questions 1–8.**

Partner B: **Go to file 7 on page 91.**

Points for answers: a = 1 point, b = 2 points, c = 3 points.
What's your score? The higher your score, the eco-friendlier you are.

1 When you see organic food, do you …
- **a** walk past it because it's too expensive?
- **b** buy something if it is on offer?
- **c** only buy organic food in the future?

2 Do you eat local food which is in season?
- **a** I don't know.
- **b** Not always, but I try.
- **c** Yes, I always do.

3 Do you walk or cycle when possible?
- **a** Only if I must.
- **b** Sometimes. To keep fit.
- **c** Yes, I'll never buy a car.

4 When you brush your teeth, do you turn off the tap?
- **a** Why? It's only for two minutes.
- **b** Yes, when I remember.
- **c** Yes, I always use a glass.

5 Do you use a cloth shopping bag?
- **a** No, it's easier to get a bag in the shop.
- **b** Yes, but I often forget to take it.
- **c** I always have one in my pocket.

6 Do you pick rubbish up off the ground?
- **a** I'd never do that!
- **b** On beaches I do.
- **c** Yes, and I put it in a rubbish bin.

7 Do you turn off the light when you are the last person to leave a room?
- **a** Why? It uses so little electricity.
- **b** I often forget.
- **c** Yes, I do it automatically.

8 In a café, if a plastic straw comes with your drink, do you …
- **a** use it anyway?
- **b** suggest they get recyclable straws?
- **c** give it back and use your own?

B **Do you need to be eco-friendlier? Think of three things you could change, take out your phone and send yourself a voice message to remind you.**

Skills practice: Describing graphs and diagrams

Diagramme machen komplexe Inhalte verständlich und überschaubar und sind deshalb bei Präsentationen hilfreich. Hier stellen wir die verschiedenen Diagramme vor.

Get it right: *Die drei wichtigsten Diagrammtypen*

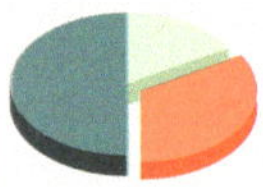

pie chart

Mit einem Tortendiagramm stellt man Anteile oder Kategorien in Prozent dar. Der volle Kreis entspricht 100 %.

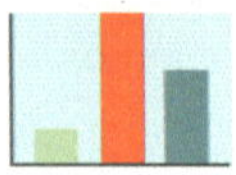

bar chart

Um Mengen oder Zahlen zu vergleichen verwendet man am besten ein Balkendiagramm.

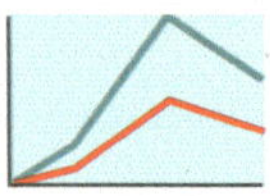

line graph

Kurvendiagramme werden benutzt, um Änderungen und Entwicklungen über einen längeren Zeitraum darzustellen. Man kann in diesem Zeitraum mehrere Werte parallel vergleichen.

A Sales graphs

A trainer is speaking to Tracy and a group of new trainees about Vegan Snacks' sales figures.

a) Match the verbs with the line graphs A, B or C.

climb ▪ decrease ▪ drop ▪ fall ▪ go up/down ▪ increase ▪ rise ▪ stay the same

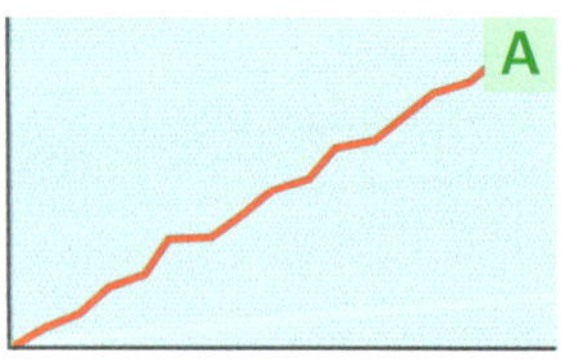

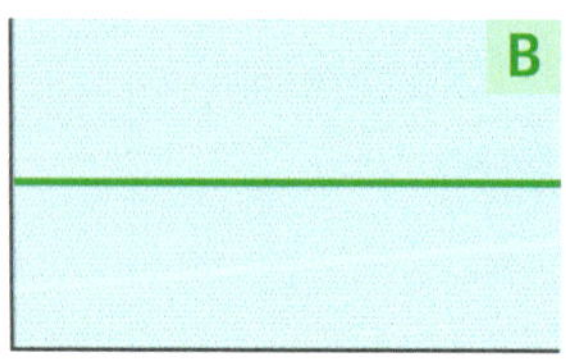

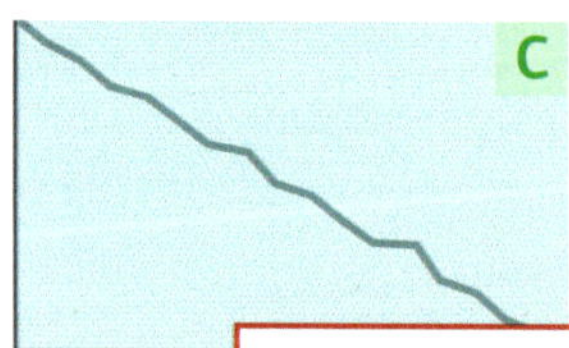

!

rise – rose – risen
fall – fell – fallen

27 **b) Listen to the trainer and then answer the questions.**

1 Is the speaker talking about graph A or graph B?

2 What were the sales figures in each quarter?

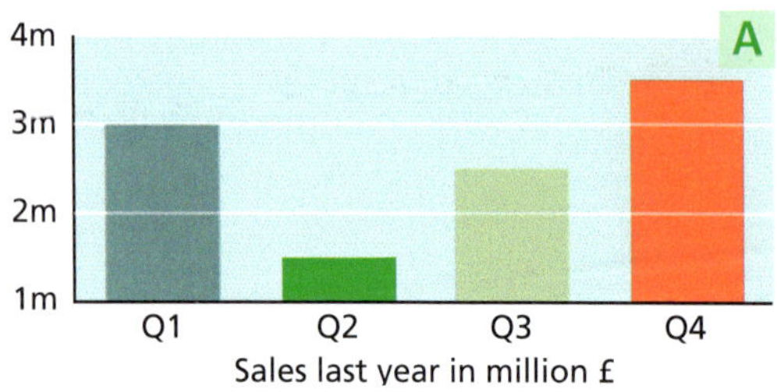

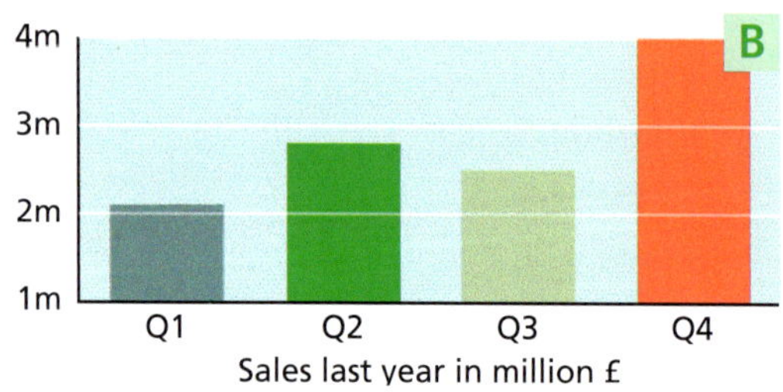

c) Listen again. Choose the right word to describe the correct graph in b).

1 Total sales increased / decreased by 10% compared with the year before.
2 In the first quarter sales rose / fell by 5% compared to the same quarter in the previous year.
3 In the UK, sales stayed the same / climbed but in Europe they increased / decreased.
4 In the second quarter sales went up / went down.
5 Third-quarter sales stayed the same / dropped compared to the previous year because of the bad summer weather.
6 Then in the fourth quarter sales rose / fell a lot because of the new stores in the USA.

B Draw and explain a graph

a) Tracy and the other trainees have the task of drawing and explaining some graphs for other vegan products. Describe your graph to your partner and draw the other graph when he/she describes it to you. Use the language in the box.
Partner A copies the left graph and then turns to file 3 on page 89.
Partner B copies the right graph and then turns to file 8 on page 92.

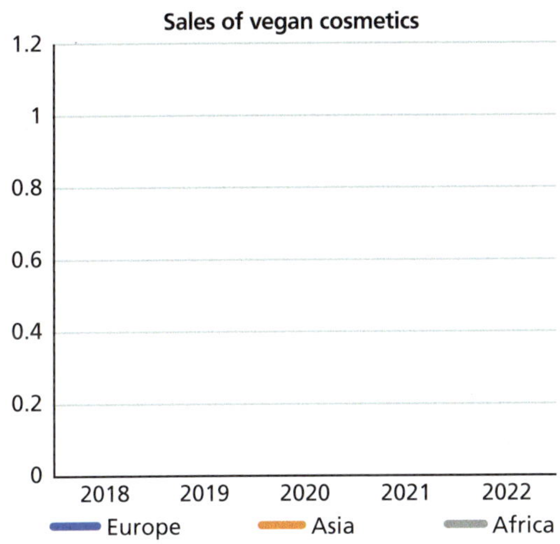

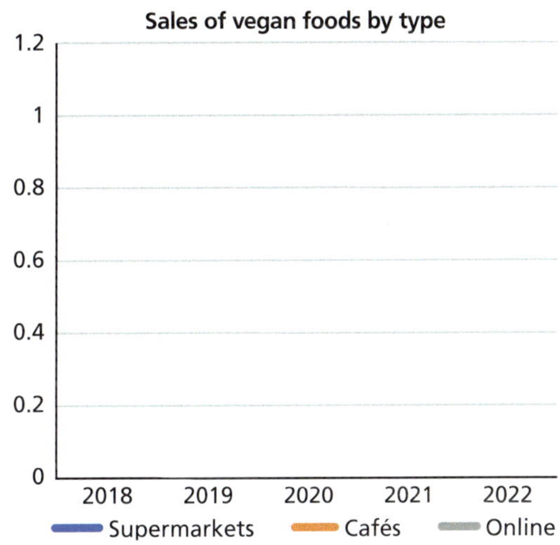

L

Describing graphs

Introduction
The graph/chart is about / clearly shows …
The figures refer to sales of … over … years.
There are three lines. The (blue) one deals with …
The vertical/horizontal axis shows …

Trends
In 20.. the percent of sales from (Asia) rose to …
Sales to (Asia) fell from … to …
They increased to … in 20 … but then decreased to … in …
Sales stayed the same from … to …

b) In class, think of possible reasons why sales might have risen or fallen.
EXAMPLE:

Maybe competition in ... became stronger.

Another point is that online shopping has become ...

Project page: Presenting arguments

You are going to do a role play and present your arguments.

A In groups of three decide what the message is in each of these posters. Do you think they work together?

You can't buy happiness, but you can buy local food.

Make friends, not food.

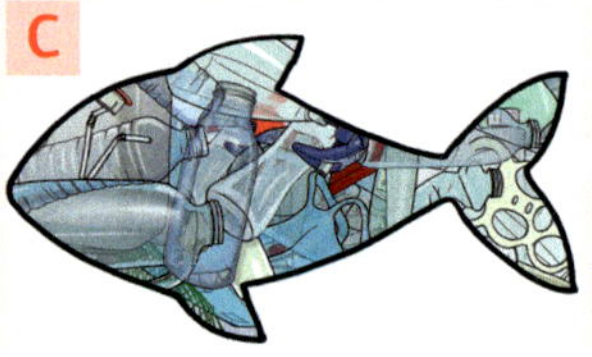

Not a healthy diet!

B Each person in the group chooses one of the posters. Write down arguments …

- to support your poster's message.
- that disagree with the messages of the other two posters.

C You are showing shoppers in your local shopping centre your poster. You want to convince the shoppers to change their habits. Do a role play in your group.

Student A: Start a conversation with two shoppers. You have one minute to talk about your ideas.

Students B and C: You are shoppers. You disagree with Student A. Say why and have a discussion.

L

Starting a conversation
Do you have a few minutes, please?
Hello. Have you heard about …?
Could I tell you about …?

Presenting the main idea
Have you ever thought …?
If you (don't) buy …, you help to support/stop …

Giving reasons
The result of people eating … is that …
… is responsible for a lot of …

Disagreeing
I see your point, but people will never …
I'm not so sure about that because …

D Act out your role play in front of the class.

E Give the other groups feedback. Say one positive thing and one negative thing about each person's contribution. Look at page 100 for some useful feedback phrases.

Snapshot

What was your favourite thing in this unit?

What important thing did you learn?

What do you need to work on?

Something went wrong … 6

Warm-up: Common complaints

Look at the situations and then complete the tasks below.

1

2

3

4

5

6

A Have you ever been in any of these situations? Tell your partner.

EXAMPLE: My new phone broke after a week.

Really, the box was broken when my new phone was delivered.

B What did you do? Who did you complain to?

C How is it best to react when something goes wrong? Talk about ideas in class.

EXAMPLE: You should stay calm.

A Writing an email to complain

Mia helps Orisa, a Nigerian refugee, write an email to her son's teacher to complain about his class.

1 Before you read

What problems do immigrant children have at school in their new country? Tell a partner.

2 Reading

28 **Read the dialogue and the email, then complete the tasks on page 57.**

Mia meets Orisa at the refugee centre in Cologne.

Mia: Let's sit and talk here.

Orisa: OK, thanks. You are always so helpful, Mia. Your English is very good. I'm sorry I can't speak German.

Mia: You mustn't worry about that. Tell me what the problem is.

Orisa: It's about Beko. He's six now and he started primary school two weeks ago. His German is good. He has two good German friends and a neighbour, who was a teacher, gives him German lessons three afternoons a week. We thought Beko should be fine.

Mia: But he wasn't fine?

Orisa: No, he wasn't. On the first day at school, they gave him a test, and he couldn't speak German. The school has put him in a special class, where they learn German in 50% of the lessons. It's not a good class, and he's very unhappy.

Mia: But why wasn't he able to speak German?

Orisa: In the summer he stayed with his cousins in Berlin, and they didn't speak any German. He was also nervous, and he forgot everything. But now he's speaking German all the time again.

Mia: I see. So how may I help?

Orisa: Well, I've written this email to his teacher to complain about the school's decision. Could you check it for me? I think there might be mistakes in it.

Dear Ms Schubert,
(1) the school's decision to put my son Beko Musa in Klasse 1A+1, the special class for students with no German.
The quick language test Beko did on the first day of school did not show how good his German is.
(2) is now in a class which is much too easy for him. He is very unhappy and wants to move to a normal class.
Beko has always played with German children and has had German lessons for the last year.
(3) badly in the test is because he spent the summer with Nigerian relatives in Berlin, where he didn't speak any German.
(4) a copy of a letter from Alfred Maier, a retired German teacher who gives Beko German lessons. He confirms that Beko speaks good basic German. (5) why the language test did not find this out.
Please review your decision as soon as possible. (6) to hearing from you.

Yours sincerely,
Orisa Musa

A **Choose the correct answer a, b or c.**

1 Beko started primary school …
- a six weeks ago.
- b three afternoons ago.
- c two weeks ago.

2 Beko forgot his German because he …
- a spoke another language all summer.
- b didn't have lessons.
- c didn't like the teacher.

B **Complete the sentences (1–6) in Orisa's email with Mia's corrections (a–f).**

- a The reason he did
- b Beko and I look forward
- c I am writing about
- d He asks the school to explain
- e As a result, he
- f I also attach

Modal verbs G

can/could	*= be able to*	*I **can** speak English.* (= kann)
may/can	*= be allowed to*	*Beko **may** visit his cousins in Berlin.* (= dürfen)
may/might	*= perhaps*	*Mia is not here yet. She **may** be late.* (= wird vielleicht)
must	*= have to*	*They **must** go to a special class.* (= müssen)
mustn't	*= not allowed to*	*You **mustn't** forget about their situation.* (= darf nicht)
should/n't	*= ought to*	*Orisa **should** learn German.* (= sollte)

3 Practice: Modal verbs

A Check it out! **Suchen Sie vier Sätze auf Seite 56 mit unterschiedlichen Modalverben.**

B **Choose the best word to complete the sentences.**

1 Why should / could / may we write to the school? We can call them.
2 I've spoken to Ms Schubert, Orisa. You mustn't / can / might call her about the details.
3 All parents could / mustn't / should feel welcome at the school.
4 If the reports are bad, it should / may / can't stop parents sending their kids to the school.
5 They could / must / might ask Beko to do another test, so he needs to practise.

4 Writing

You went on an English course in Oxford. In the school brochure it said:

- Lessons only take place in the mornings, with the afternoons free for sightseeing.
- Classes have no more than 12 students.
- All teachers are British native speakers.

But when you arrived, you found the description was false:

- There were afternoon lessons three days a week.
- Your class had 18 students in a very small classroom.
- Two of your teachers were from Malaysia.

Write an email to the school manager, Ms Snow, to complain.
☆ **Turn to page 97.**

B Finding solutions

When Ms Schubert reads Orisa Musa's email, she phones her.

Video
Watch the video and look at page 87 for more information about dealing with customer complaints.

1 Listening

Listen to the recording. Are these statements true or false? Correct the false statements.

29

1 Orisa calls Ms Schubert.
2 Beko's teacher says Beko's German is good.
3 Beko speaks a lot in class.
4 The school plans to test Beko's German again on Thursday.
5 Orisa will go to the school on Thursday.

2 Replying to a complaint

Work with a partner. Read Ms Schubert's reply to another parent's complaint. The sentences (a–i) are in the wrong order. Write the letter with the sentences in the best order.

a Ms Späth is ill at the moment, but she will call you next week.
b Dear Ms Fatić,
c She would like to arrange a meeting to discuss things as soon as possible.
d However, we will do everything we can to help Esma feel happier at school.
e I've spoken to her teacher and she thinks Esma may like to change where she sits in class.
f Your sincerely,
Bettina Schubert
g They surprised us because the other children seem to really enjoy the class.
h We are very sorry to hear about your daughter Esma's complaints about her new class.
i Feedback from parents is always important to us and we work hard to find solutions.

G

The will future for decisions when you are speaking

Das *will*-Futur wird auch verwendet, wenn etwas im Moment des Sprechens entschieden wird.

Aussage	Verneinung
Can I speak to Ms Schubert, please?	*How about meeting on Friday afternoon?*
– She isn't here now. I ***will*** *ask her to call you back.*	*– OK. I* ***won't*** *plan anything else for then.*

3 Practice: Will future for decisions when you are speaking

30

A Check it out! **Hören Sie einen Teil der Aufnahme noch einmal und schreiben Sie die zwei Beispiele von *will future for decisions when you are speaking* auf.**

B **Complete the sentences with the verbs from the box and the will future.**

find ■ have to ■ help ■ not catch ■ open ■ sit

1 The child is crying. I ___ with him.
2 She can't see. I ___ someone to help.
3 They're sad. We ___ do something.
4 We're late. We ___ the film.
5 It is so hot. I ___ the window.
6 That bag is heavy. I ___ you with it.

☆ **Turn to page 98.**

4 Words, words, words: Complaining

A Copy the table and put the phrases in the correct column.

I'm afraid I have a complaint to make. ▪ We do everything we can to …
I understand how you feel, but … ▪ I want to complain about … ▪ I expect an apology.
I'm very sorry to hear that … ▪ Please accept my apologies. ▪ Let me explain why …

Making a complaint	Answering a complaint
I'm afraid I have a complaint to make.	*We do everything we can to …*

B Work with a partner. Each of you think of three things you want to complain about. Partner A makes his/her complaints. Partner B answers the complaints. Then swap roles.

EXAMPLE: *I want to complain about these flowers I bought for my mum. Half of them are dead!*
– Please accept my apologies. I'll get some fresh ones.

5 Pairwork: A role play

Work with a partner. Partner A is in a park. Partner B has just stood up from a bench to go back to work after having his/her lunch. He/She has left his/her rubbish on the bench. Role play the conversation. The phrases in exercise 4 can help. When you finish, swap roles.

Partner A	Partner B
Fragen Sie, ob B weiß, dass er/sie etwas auf der Bank vergessen hat.	
	Sie wissen es. Sie müssen aber zurück im Büro für eine Besprechung.
Das können Sie gut verstehen, aber auf der Bank liegt viel Müll.	
	Sagen Sie A, dass es Arbeiter/innen im Park gibt, die sauber machen.
Sagen Sie, dass die Arbeiter/innen im Park nicht regelmäßig arbeiten.	
	Sie müssen jetzt wirklich zurück im Büro.
Fragen Sie, ob B den Mülleimer gesehen hat.	
	Sie hatten ihn nicht gesehen, aber jetzt.
Bedanken Sie sich bei B.	

C Cultural misunderstandings

Mia wants to find out more about cultural differences and finds a good website.

1 Reading

31 **Read the two posts on the website 'Comparing Cultures', then complete the tasks below.**

I'm Chinese. I live with my German boyfriend, Sven. Sometimes cultural differences make things difficult! I like to cook lots of small dishes for dinner, but Sven prefers just one or two. It's the Chinese way.
Last weekend, Bai, a friend from Beijing came to stay. The first thing she did was walk around the house and look at everything. Sven was a bit upset, but I explained that this is normal in China. Bai brought us a bowl of fruit as a present and *two* bottles of wine. Sven was surprised. "We're not in hospital! And I'm not an alcoholic," he said. I explained that fruit is a very common present in China, and that we like to give presents in pairs because 'two' is a lucky number.
When I said goodbye to Bai at the station, Sven was shocked again. We seemed so 'cold'. We didn't show any emotion. But that's normal in China, even if you know you won't see somebody for a long time.
Barbara Uan, Hamburg

I'm from London. My mum is German, and I always wanted to work in Germany. After college I got a job in Stuttgart. I can speak German, but I still had a hard time. I started work at 9, but my boss – like many Germans – started early, at 7:30, and he wanted me to do the same. Germans, as I learned, are very punctual. Never be late for a meeting! But don't be too early either, because there's not much small talk before it. A meeting is just a meeting. In the UK people like to joke and have a little fun at work. Not here. Work is work. You are friendly with your colleagues, but they aren't really your friends. When I wanted to meet some colleagues for a drink after work, nobody was interested. They just wanted to get home. So, did I adapt? Yes, I began to enjoy the differences. In fact, with the German influence, I have become a better, more efficient worker. But I also keep my British side. I try not to plan too much and I'm flexible. I'm not always too serious and try to see the funny side of situations. It's nice feeling at home in two cultures.
Ulrich Clark, Stuttgart

A **Work with a partner. What do you know about Barbara and Ulrich? Tell each other the facts.** EXAMPLE: *Barbara lives in Hamburg.*

B **Complete the sentences.**

1 It's the Chinese way to
2 'Two' is a lucky number in China, so
3 Before a meeting in Germany, there
4 In Germany people separate

C **Work with a partner.**
Partner A: Tell B about the cultural differences between China and Germany.
EXAMPLE: *In China they cook lots of small dishes, but in Germany …*
Partner B: Tell A five things which were new for Ulrich in Germany.
EXAMPLE: *Ulrich wanted to start work at 9 o'clock, but his German boss …*

☆ **Turn to page 98.**

2 Mediation

Read another text on the website 'Comparing Cultures', then do the task below.

32

If you have contact with people from other countries, you need to understand their culture so that you can avoid misunderstandings. Here are just a few examples of differences from around the world.

Japan

- Nodding the head is important to show that you understand the other person when they are speaking.
- Don't use the word 'no'. The Japanese avoid it and often use 'yes': *Shall we have dinner? – Yes, I'd like that, but I already have plans.*

India

- Never refuse food. Your host may find it insulting. But don't feel you have to finish all the food on your plate.
- Some people eat with their hands. Use only your right hand and your first three fingers and the thumb.

France

- Don't expect to find a restaurant if your meeting ends at 3 p.m. or after 10 p.m. The French have quite strict times for meals.
- Always start a conversation with a greeting – *bonjour* or just *hello*. It's rude not to.

Brazil

- Brazilians stand closer together when they talk than people in many other cultures, and they often touch the other person.
- Brazilians speak Portuguese. You may offend them if you speak Spanish.

Italy

- Don't be upset if people are a little late. It's not a priority for Italians to be punctual.
- Think about what you wear. Clothes are important to Italians.

Russia

- Don't smile or laugh too much. Smiling isn't as polite as it is in western countries.
- Don't be surprised if nobody smiles in shops or hotels. In meetings, laughing or smiling a lot is disrespectful.

Ein Freund / Eine Freundin hat folgende Aufgabe zum Thema ‚Interkulturelle Unterschiede' in der Schule bekommen. Sie finden sie interessant. Schreiben Sie die Lösungen in ganzen Sätzen.

In welchem Land waren diese Personen? Begründen Sie Ihre Antwort.

1 „In der Besprechung hat niemand gelacht. Alle waren sehr ernst."
2 „Ich habe lange gewartet und als sie kamen, haben sie meinen Anzug kritisch angeguckt!"
3 „Es war komisch, dass alle ständig genickt haben."
4 „Unsere Besprechung ging sehr lang. Danach gab es kein offenes Restaurant mehr."
5 "Ich erzählte auf Spanisch, was ich vorhatte. Aber das wollten sie nicht hören."

3 Words, words, words: Cultural misunderstandings

Look at the text above and find the English for these German words.

1 Nicken
2 beleidigend
3 streng
4 unhöflich
5 beleidigen
6 pünktlich
7 respektlos

Skills practice: Speaking English

Sie befinden sich in einer Situation, in der ausschließlich Englisch gesprochen wird? Kein Grund zur Panik! Hier sind ein paar Tipps, wie Sie jede Situation meistern können.

Get it right: *Wie kommuniziere ich mit Menschen, die wenig Englisch sprechen?*

- Merken Sie sich ein paar höfliche Ausdrücke (‚Danke' oder ‚Guten Morgen'). So bauen Sie Vertrauen auf.
- Überlegen Sie, bevor Sie sprechen: Wählen Sie einfache Wörter und kurze Erklärungen.
- Sprechen Sie klar und deutlich, aber nicht laut, sondern freundlich.
- Sprechen Sie langsam. Machen Sie Pausen zwischen Sätzen, damit die Person Zeit hat, den Inhalt ganz zu verstehen. Das gibt auch Ihnen Zeit, Ihren nächsten Satz vorzubereiten.
- Benutzen Sie Körpersprache. Manche Aussagen lassen sich durch Mimik und Gestik leichter darstellen.

A How to say things simpler

a) Mia is talking to the people in the refugee centre about things they didn't understand. Replace the bold expressions in the sentences with the simpler words on the right.

1	**Get a move on!** We're late.	a	to wait
2	I've lost my **hairdryer**. Can you help me?	b	I don't like
3	My friend asked me **to hang on a minute**.	c	Walk faster!
4	**What's up**? You haven't eaten anything.	d	Is everything OK?
5	I **can't stand** the music she listens to.	e	thing for drying my hair

b) The immigrants who Mia helps speak very little English and often ask Mia questions. Make Mia's answers simpler. There is too much information in Mia's answers.

Mia: Hello, Meena. Do you have any questions?
Meena: Yes. I want a job. Where can I look?
Mia: (0) Look at this special job website designed for immigrants.
EXAMPLE: *Look at this job website. It is for immigrants.*
Meena: What about qualifications?
Mia: The 'qualifications' part of the website tells you what qualifications you need.
(1)
Meena: OK. I want to learn German? Where can I do this?
Mia: We have German classes here every afternoon. There are different classes depending on how much German you already know.
(2)
Meena: OK. My daughter is sick. Where is there a doctor?
Mia: This is a list of doctors who help young children. These ones speak English.
(3)
Meena: I miss my family. When can they come here?
Mia: I can't answer that question. I can look for someone who has more information.
(4)

B Understanding signs

a) There are lots of important signs in the refugee centre. Everyone needs to understand them. Match these signs with their correct translation.

1

Vorsicht Rutschgefahr!

2

Nachtruhe ab 21:00 Uhr

3

Hier keine Kinderwagen abstellen!

4

Öffnungszeiten Büro

5

Bitte Spülmaschine einräumen.

6
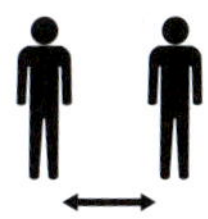
Abstand halten!

a Keep your distance!
b Don't leave prams here!
c Please load the dishwasher.
d Quiet please from 9 p.m.
e Office opening hours
f Caution: Slippery!

b) Work with a partner. Explain in English what the signs tell you.

> Wenn Sie für jemanden dolmetschen, ist es meistens nicht nötig, Wort für Wort zu übersetzen. Es reicht, den Sinn wiederzugeben.

C Mediating

In Mia's nursery school one of the English parents has a problem. Mia is talking to the parent and one of her colleagues who is also trying to help. Mediate between Mr Sands and Gabi.

You: Mr Sands, tell me about your problem again, please and I'll translate for Gabi.
Mr Sands: OK. Yesterday, my son Simon didn't feel very well.
You: **(0)** *Seinem Sohn ging es gestern nicht gut.*
Mr Sands: He told me that he started crying as he felt sick.
You: **(1 auf Deutsch)**
Gabi: Ja, das habe ich gesehen und bin direkt zu ihm gegangen. Leider hatte er sich schon übergeben.
You: **(2 auf Englisch)**
Mr Sands: He told me that. Where was the other nursery assistant? He was really upset when I picked him up.
You: **(3 auf Deutsch)**
Gabi: Das tut mir leid. Ein anderes Kind war gleichzeitig krank. Ich habe mich sofort um Simon gekümmert.
You: **(4 auf Englisch)**
Mr Sands: Thanks. Maybe he overreacted because he didn't feel well. He was happy to come this morning. I just wanted to check what had happened.
You: **(5 auf Deutsch)**

Project page: Giving feedback

You are going to design a feedback form to use in class.

A What is important

Work in a small group. Make a list of what is important when you give a presentation.

B Designing the form

Look at the list you made in A. How can you rate these things? Think about the best way.

- Give points from 1-5
- From most important to least important
- From 'well done' to 'needs improving'
- Use smilies

C Other details

Don't forget you need to know who did the presentation, when it was and what it was about. One form for more presentations might be good if you want to compare them. Don't forget to leave space so you can add comments too.

D Do a gallery walk.

E Give feedback to the other groups. Look at page 100 for some useful feedback phrases. Which feedback form is best?

Giving feedback L

😊	😐	🙁
■ The design is very clear. ■ The list covers everything. ■ The rating system works.	■ The structure is clear. ■ I would add … to the list. ■ I think … would be better	■ Sorry, but it looks a bit messy. ■ There are some important things missing in the list. ■ You forgot to include …

Snapshot

What was your favourite thing in this unit?	What important thing did you learn?	What do you need to work on?

Meeting up in Canada 7

Warm-up: Telephone language

A **What phone calls do you make? Are they all to family and friends or do you make other phone calls? Look at the situations in the pictures for ideas.**

33 **B** **Listen to the two short dialogues. Which photo on the right matches which dialogue? Discuss your reasons with a partner.**

EXAMPLE:

I think the top photo matches dialogue … because …

I disagree. I think …

C **Listen to the two dialogues again. Match each phrase to the correct dialogue. Which dialogue is a formal phone call?**

Have you got a minute? ▪ Hold on a minute, [name]. ▪ What's up? Thank you, [name]. ▪ Great idea! ▪ Can I help you? Can I check my diary a minute? ▪ See you then.

D **Practise a short business call with a partner. Use the right phrases from C. Swap roles.**

A: Good morning. West Garage, *[Ihr Name]* speaking. (1)

B: Good morning, *[As Name]*. This is *[Ihr Name]*. My *[brakes/lights]* are broken. When have you got a free appointment, please?

A: (2) OK, would *[Datum/Uhrzeit]* work for you?

B: (3) Yes, that sounds fine.

A: Great, *[Bs Name]*. Then I'll write that in the diary.

B: (4) I'll see you on *[Datum]* at *[Uhrzeit]*.

A: Great, *[Bs Name]*. Goodbye.

B: Goodbye.

A Making arrangements and appointments

Tracy is working on a project that tests food packaging. She is going to Packex, a trade fair in Toronto. It's a chance to meet Jamal. Mia is going to be on holiday in Canada and will meet them.

1 Before you read

If a friend who lives in another town visited you, what would you do on the first day?

2 Reading

34 **A Listen to part of a phone call between the friends before they meet in Toronto. Then read the phone call text below and listen again. There are small differences which are underlined below. Correct the differences. Find two more differences which are not underlined.**

Jamal: You're both coming to Toronto!

Tracy: I'm *so* looking forward to it.

Jamal: What are your plans? I won't be at the fair. I'm very busy in the office. You're going to land on Tuesday afternoon, right?

Tracy: Yes. I have non-stop meetings and workshops until Friday afternoon. Why don't we meet for a drink after work on Thursday?

Mia: I could join you on Thursday too. I fly in that afternoon. There'll be Wi-Fi at the airport. I'll message you when I land.

Jamal: And on Friday evening the weekend starts! I'm going to take you to my uncle's restaurant. Have you ever eaten Swiss food?

Mia: No, never. But I've heard it's spicy. What are we going to do on Saturday and Sunday? The CN Tower looks amazing.

Jamal: How about going to Niagara Falls? It's close. We could do a day trip.

Mia: When's your flight back, Tracy?

Tracy: Early on Saturday evening. You two decide what we're going to do. I'm OK with everything.

Mia: Would it be possible to go to Niagara Falls on Saturday and then the CN Tower on Sunday morning?

Jamal: Yes, let's do that. Then Tracy has plenty of time to get to the airport. What about you, Mia? How long are you going to stay in Canada?

Mia: Well actually, on Sunday evening I'm going to take the train from Toronto to Montreal, across the Rocky Mountains. It'll take three days! I'm going to fly back to Frankfurt from Vancouver.

Tracy: Wow! I wish I could come too. But isn't it expensive?

Mia: No, the price for business class was OK. First we're going to have fun in Toronto.

Jamal: That's right. On Saturday night, we can eat the best burgers in town and then go to a jazz club.

Mia: Cool. Do you think we could have brunch somewhere on Sunday?

Jamal: Good idea. I'll find a place with a view over the lake.

B Beantworte diese Fragen auf Deutsch.

1 Warum kann Jamal nicht zur Messe gehen?
2 Wann kommt Mia in Toronto an?
3 Was schlagen Mia und Jamal fürs Wochenende vor?
4 Was macht Mia nach dem Wochenende?
5 Was möchte Mia am Sonntag machen?

C Decide whether these statements are true or false. Correct the false statements.

1 Jamal and Tracy are going to meet after work on Wednesday. *False, they are going to …*
2 Mia is going to contact the others from Toronto airport.
3 They decide to pay a quick visit to Niagara Falls on Sunday morning.
4 Jamal has two things planned for Saturday evening.
5 Jamal's uncle has a burger restaurant.

G

The *going to* future …

wird für Absichten und Pläne verwendet.

to meet (treffen)

Aussage	Frage	Verneinung
*We **are going to meet** in town.*	***Is** Mia **going to meet** us?*	***I'm not going to meet** you.*

3 Practice: Going to future

A Check it out! Find three examples of the *going to* future in the text on page 66. Look at the sentences. What do you need for the *going to* future?

B Complete these sentences with verbs from the box and the *going to* future.

go ▪ introduce ▪ show ▪ not stay ▪ travel ▪ not visit

1 Jamal, Tracy and Mia ___ to the CN Tower.
2 Tracy ___ as long as Mia in Canada.
3 Mia ___ more than 2,000 miles on the train.
4 ___ Jamal ___ Mia and Tracy to his uncle?
5 Mia ___ Montreal.
6 ___ you ___ us your office, Jamal?

☆ Turn to page 98.

4 Making suggestions

A Find these phrases in the text on page 66. Which three aren't in the text?

Let's … ▪ Would it be possible …? ▪ Perhaps you should … ▪ How about… (-ing)?
Do you think we could …? ▪ You could … ▪ Why don't we …? ▪ Should we …?

B Work in small groups. Use the phrases from A to make suggestions about these things:

1 making a lot of money
2 going on holiday
3 starting your own business
4 getting fit
5 improving your English
6 finding an apprenticeship

EXAMPLE:

How about going to visit my family in Italy?

B Changing plans

Tracy had a great time in Toronto, but her return journey didn't work out as planned.

1 Before you read

Look at these things that housekeepers find in hotel rooms after guests have left. Which do you think they find most often: A, B or C? What other things do people forget?

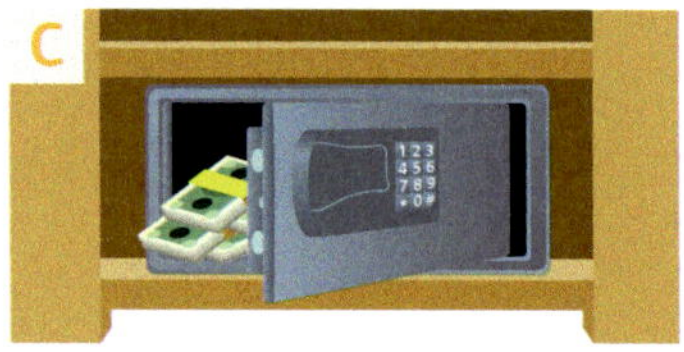

2 Reading

Read the dialogue, then complete the tasks below.
35

Operator: Lake View Hotel. Can I help you?
Tracy: Hello. I left something in my room this morning when I left.
Operator: I'll put you through to reception.
Nuna: Reception. Nuna speaking. I understand you left something in your room.
Tracy: Yes, a new tablet. It was in the safe.
Nuna: Don't worry. We usually find these things. Could I have your name and the dates you stayed with us?
Tracy: My name's Tracy Black. I had a single room for four nights. I checked in on the 12th.
Nuna: One moment please. I'll just check that. You were in room 2024, and you checked out this morning.
Tracy: That's correct.
Nuna: I'll just ask the housekeeper if she has found anything. One moment. ... She's found it!
Tracy: Oh, that's good news!
Nuna: What would you like us to do with it? We can send it, but I'm afraid there will be a charge.
Tracy: I'm calling you from the airport. I'm really early. If I take the train, I expect I'll arrive at Lake View in less than an hour. That gives me just enough time to get the tablet and be back for my flight.
Nuna: OK. The tablet will be here at reception. I'm going off duty now, but I'll inform my colleague.
Tracy: Thank you so much for your help.
Nuna: You're welcome.

A What's the connection between the photos and the dialogue?

B Complete the sentences.

1 Tracy left her ___ in ___
2 Tracy had stayed in ___
3 Tracy ___ at Lake View in less than ___
4 She isn't going to see Nuna because ___

☆ **Turn to page 98.**

3 Listening

It takes Tracy longer than expected to get back to the airport. She thinks she is going to miss her flight, so she calls the airline.

A Match the English words to their German meanings.

1 seat	**5** gate	**9** cancel
2 boarding pass	**6** security	**10** free
3 on time	**7** available	
4 delay	**8** fee	

Bordkarte ▪ Flugsteig ▪ Sitzplatz
kostenlos ▪ pünktlich
Sicherheitskontrolle ▪ verfügbar
stornieren ▪ Gebühr ▪ Verspätung

36

B Now listen to Tracy's phone call and choose the right answer (a, b or c) to complete the sentences.

1 Tracy already has her ___ for the flight to London.
a passport **b** bags **c** boarding pass

2 Her flight is ___
a CA9 at 6:30. **b** A9 at 5:30. **c** CA9 at 11:00.

3 The flight is ___
a 20 minutes late. **b** on time. **c** closed.

4 There are seats available in ___
a economy. **b** business. **c** economy and business.

5 Tracy's bags are going to ___
a stay in Toronto. **b** travel with her. **c** go on the first flight.

!

in	on	at
in 2021	**on** Friday	**at** 9:00
in May		**at** night
in an hour		

C Have you ever missed a plane, train or bus? Tell your neighbour what happened.

4 Words, words, words: Prepositions with times

Fill in the missing prepositions.

1 I have a seat on the flight ___ 15:30.
2 The gate closes ___ 20 minutes.
3 There is a second flight later today ___ 19:30.
4 I really need to be at work ___ Monday.

5 Pairwork: A role play

Partner A: Read your role card, prepare what to say in English and then call the hotel.
Partner B: Go to file 9 on page 92.

Partner A role card

Sie haben Ihre Sonnenbrille nach einem Aufenthalt im Queen's Hotel im Zimmer vergessen. Sie rufen das Hotel von zu Hause an. Sie haben folgende Informationen zur Hand:

- Ihren Name und Ihre Anschrift
- wann Ihr Aufenthalt im Hotel war sowie Ihre Zimmernummer
- eine Beschreibung der Sonnenbrille
- eine Vermutung, wo Sie sie vergessen haben

☆ **Turn to page 98/99.**

C Living in Canada

Mia listens to a podcast of young Canadians talking about their lives on her train journey from Toronto to Vancouver.

Video 7

Watch the video and look at page 88 for more information about Canada.

1 Before you read

What do you know about Canada? Think about these things.

- Cities
- Animals and nature
- Climate and weather
- Sights and things to do

2 Reading

37 **A Read the texts, then find the underlined places on the map on page 66 or 122.**

A I'm from Yellowknife in northern Canada. It's a huge territory, but only about 40,000 people live here. My grandfather was a whale hunter, but now my family works in the city – I'm an apprentice electrician. This is the sunniest place in Canada, we call it the Land of the Midnight Sun. It doesn't get dark for six weeks in the summer. That's when I love canoeing to my favourite island and back in daylight at 3 a.m. Winter, on the other hand, is another story! For months the average temperature is about -25°C. There's lots to do here. I often go ice fishing on the lake with friends. Another friend has a dog team and we go sledding every weekend. I wouldn't want to live anywhere else. *Kallik (19)*

B Bonjour! Living in Montreal is like living in New York and Paris at the same time. The city is completely bilingual, like all of the province of Quebec – there is a city and a province called Quebec, by the way. French is the official language here, so it helps if you can speak a little French. Because of the French influence, the food here is amazing. We have thousands of great French restaurants. I'm sure that's why I decided to become a chef. There's a lot of friendly competition between Montreal and one of Canada's other big cities, Toronto, especially in sport. Winter sports are really popular, and hockey is our national sport. (We call it just hockey, not 'ice' hockey.) *Marie (20)*

C My family immigrated from Hong Kong to Calgary, Alberta, five years ago. Alberta is a beautiful province, with the famous Rocky Mountains in the north and west, and hundreds of miles of flat prairies in the south. There are plenty of good jobs in the oil industry. You also meet people from so many different countries. Everyone is really open, friendly and patient. People explain things if you don't understand. Having the Rocky Mountains on our doorstep is absolutely amazing! We have all learned to ski and the glaciers and lakes are just beautiful. If you are lucky you might see bears in the mountains too. You have to be careful though and remember it's their home you are visiting. We're really happy we moved here. I got my Business Administration qualification last month and tomorrow I'm going for an interview at a Calgary hospital. *Lin (19)*

B **Choose the best title for texts A, B and C. There is one more title than you need.**

1 The job capital of Canada
2 Lakes, mountains and glaciers
3 Short nights and cold months
4 One city, two cultures

C **Read these sentences. Who do you think could have said them – Kallik, Marie or Lin?**

1 You need French and English to get a job.
2 There's lots to do in winter.
3 My parents found a job within six months.
4 Our way of life has changed.
5 I hope to open my own restaurant.

3 Words, words, words: Describing a new country

Choose the right words to complete the sentences.

1 The northern / north part of Canada gets very cold.
2 The territory / plain is not famous / popular for people to immigrate / immigration to.
3 The first immigration / immigrants to Canada were the French and the English.
4 They have learned to exchange / adapt and live together.
5 There is competition / competitors between Canadian cities to attract new arrivals.
6 Officially / Official figures show that Toronto has the highest number of new arrivals every year.

4 Mediation

Read these things you should know about Canada, then complete the task.

Things you should know about Canada

- Canada is huge.
- There are three Canadian cities in the top ten most liveable cities in the world: Vancouver, Toronto and Calgary.
- More than 20% of Canadians were born in another country.
- There are two official languages: French and English.
- The cities are good but the area between them is even better: prairies, lakes, …
- Canadians love ice hockey – even on the frozen lakes in winter.
- Canadians' favourite foods are poutine and maple syrup – but not together!
- The Canadians designed their national flag – that is why they all love it.
- 'Sorry' is the most popular word in Canada – Canadians love apologizing to each other.

Sie finden diese Informationen interessant und möchten Ihren Freund / Ihre Freundin davon erzählen. Fassen Sie die fünf interessantesten Punkte zusammen.

5 It's your turn

A **Research one of these places on the internet, then write a short description of it.**

The Chilkoot Trail, Yukon **Toronto, Ontario** **Baffin Island, Nunavut**

☆ **Turn to page 99.**

B **Read your description to your partner. Don't say the name of the place. Can they guess it?**

Skills practice: Writing the minutes of a meeting

Wenn man an Besprechungen teilnimmt, ist man irgendwann einmal dran, Protokoll zu führen. Das macht niemand besonders gern, aber es gehört dazu und ist weniger schlimm, als man denkt.

Get it right: *Was ist bei einem Protokoll wichtig?*

Was auf jeden Fall in einem Protokoll sein muss:

- Datum und Uhrzeit der Besprechung
- Namen aller Teilnehmende/n – auch derjenigen, die eingeladen waren, aber nicht teilnehmen konnten
- Anlass der Besprechung
- Tagesordnungspunkte und besprochene Themen
- Entscheidungen, die in der Besprechung getroffen wurden, und wer was bis wann erledigen soll
- Datum und Uhrzeit der Folgebesprechung
- Unterlagen, auf die in der Besprechung verwiesen wurde

A Making notes

While Tracy was in Canada, she attended a meeting with her boss and some Canadian colleagues. She was asked to write the minutes of the meeting.

Look at Tracy's notes from her meeting. Use the list of things above that are needed in the minutes of a meeting and decide which things in Tracy's notes she needs to write in the minutes.

Thursday's meeting

When:	*Thursday May 14th, 2:30 p.m.*
Where:	*Room 100, Red Tower*
Participants:	*Tracy (me), Steve Dyer (Toronto), Mark Stevens (Liverpool), Clare James (Liverpool), Sarah Bleu (Toronto); missing* **(1)** *Davis (sick, Toronto)*
Reason for the meeting:	*Packex + packaging inventions, Clare Dyer called meeting*
Packex:	*busy,* **(2)** *conversations,* **(3)**
New innovations (Paul Stevens):	*new food packaging machine,* **(4)** *Sun is shining outside – call Jamal* *Organize meeting with Packfast machine company, come from Germany, paper not plastic*
Next meeting:	*May 30th, 9:00 a.m., Liverpool, invite participants from today + Anna Philips and Greg Davis*
Send:	*specifications of Packfast machine, photos of Packex, menu from canteen*

B Checking your notes

a) **Tracy still had some jetlag at the meeting. Compare her notes with the agenda. What mistakes has she made? Make a list.**

Meeting agenda

Date: Thurs, May 13 **Time**: 1:30 p.m. **Room:** 150

1:30 p.m.	Introduction
1:45 p.m.	First impressions of Packex – group feedback
2:30 p.m.	COFFEE
2:45 p.m.	New packaging innovations – Paul Stevens
3:45 p.m.	COFFEE
4:00 p.m.	Questions + answers – new innovations
5:00 p.m.	End of meeting

38 b) **Listen to part of Tracy's meeting. What has she missed in her notes?**

C Work with a partner.

Use Tracy's corrected notes to write the minutes of the meeting. Look for examples of minutes on the internet to help you with the structure.

D Check your minutes

Compare your minutes with another pair. Did you remember everything? Add anything you missed out.

Get it right: *CHECKLISTE*

- ☑ Besprechungsnotizen gelesen und verstanden?
- ☑ Rückfragen geklärt?
- ☑ Protokoll geschrieben?
- ☑ Am nächsten Tag in Ruhe durchgelesen?
- ☑ Protokoll überarbeitet? Korrektur gelesen?
- ☑ Rückmeldungen eingeholt und Protokoll erneut verbessert?
- ☑ An alle Teilnehmer versenden! Anlagen anhängen!

Project page: Entertaining visitors

When Tracy was in Toronto, she spent an afternoon with her Canadian colleagues. Work in a small group and prepare a programme for some foreign visitors to your school.

A Work with a partner. Imagine there is a group of foreign visitors coming to your school. What things would you like to do with them or show them? Make a list.

Ideas of things to do:
Eat local food
...
...

B Now join another pair. Prepare the programme for the group of visitors. Make sure there are a number of different options.

	Wednesday	Thursday	Friday
Morning	Lessons	Lessons	
Afternoon	Group arrives (4 p.m.)	Lessons (until 4:30 p.m.)	
Evening			Group departs (6:30 p.m.)

- Copy the schedule above and highlight the days and times when the group has free time.
- Decide the things you would like to do with the visitors in their free time. Add them to the schedule.
- Plan the details: How will you get there? How much time will you spend there? Where will you eat?

EXAMPLE:

The first thing they need to do/see is ...

It's important to show them ...

Those who are tired may want ...

I'm not sure that will interest them because ...

C Present your programme to the class.

- Choose one person in your group to introduce the programme.
- Choose different people to present each activity and to say why you have chosen it.

D Ask the class if they have any further suggestions or feedback on your ideas. Look at page 100 for some useful feedback phrases.

Snapshot

What was your favourite thing in this unit?

What important thing did you learn?

What do you need to work on?

My first salary 8

Warm-up: How am I going to spend it?

A It's a great feeling seeing your first salary in your bank account. What are you going to do with the money you earn every month? Make a 'My first salary' poster like the example below. Add the phrases from the box or use your own ideas.

buy a VR-headset ▪ get a credit card ▪ finance a car
give parents a big present ▪ hire a personal trainer
get my own flat ▪ own a horse ▪ take singing lessons
learn to fly a plane ▪ save my salary

B Work with a partner. Tell your partner about your poster and listen to them explain their poster. Give your partner feedback:

- What do you like? What isn't a good idea? Why?
- What things haven't they thought about?
- Is something missing?

C Tell the class. Who has the most surprising plans?

EXAMPLE: Nathan is going to give his parents a fantastic present and then ask if they can help him with financing a car.

That's not a good idea because ...

I would/wouldn't ... because ...

A Paying for your dreams

Jamal, Tracy and Mia are having a video call about their plans now that they're all earning money.

1 Before you read

What advice would you ask your parents for when you get your first salary? Talk to a partner.

2 Reading

39 **Read the dialogue, then complete the tasks.**

Mia: Every time I visit my parents these days, they start talking about financial planning! Now that I earn a salary, they want me to budget the money I spend. They talk about insurance and ask about my long-term financial goals. But that's not what I want. I'm just too young to plan my life like that. I want to spend my money and see the world. At the moment I'm saving for an all-inclusive holiday in the sun.

Jamal: Wow, that's exciting. I saved most of my first three months' money in a savings account which I call my 'emergency fund'. It feels good to know it's there. This is my dream: I want a good kitchen that my girlfriend and I can use to cook great Syrian food. Don't laugh! There are thousands of us who are missing home cooking here in Toronto. We'll advertise our food on social media, where we'll also find customers who will hopefully give us feedback and ideas. We want to own a business and have fun at the same time. We need a much better kitchen though, and that will cost money. We are both saving, making plans and collecting recipes.

Tracy: It's a great way to keep in touch with your culture. And your food is amazing. I remember that great meal we had at your uncle's restaurant.

Mia: Maybe somebody will buy your business for millions! How about you, Tracy? Do you have any dreams?

Tracy: Well, the first thing I wanted when I started work was a car. I was tired of taking the bus everywhere. I dreamt of driving to work in a shiny new car. When I looked at the costs, I got a shock. I needed to borrow money. I knew that, because I couldn't pay cash. But I couldn't afford more than 20% of my salary for the monthly payments. That just wasn't enough for a new car. Then there were the other costs: insurance, petrol, maintenance, etc. So, I have to be realistic. Now I'm going to buy a used car and hope it won't need any expensive repairs, and my long-term goal is to buy a new one. I don't know about you, but as a student my parents gave me money and I never thought about what I spent it on. Now I look closely at the money I spend.

Mia: I know exactly what you mean, Tracy. But for me it's still a great feeling to have my own money.

A **Name one thing each that Mia, Jamal and Tracy are going to do with their salaries?**

B Decide whether these statements are true or false. Correct the false ones.

1 Mia's parents just want her to enjoy life.
2 Jamal has saved some money for emergencies.
3 Tracy expects to pay a quarter of her salary for a car loan.

G

Relative pronouns …
brauchen Sie, um Personen oder Sachen genauer zu beschreiben.
- *who* wird verwendet, um Personen näher zu beschreiben.

Mia is the friend ***who*** *likes to travel.*
- *which* wird verwendet, um Dinge oder Tiere näher zu beschreiben.

The car ***which*** *Tracy would like to buy is three years old.*

! *who* und *which* können beide durch *that* ersetzt werden.

3 Practice: Relative pronouns

A Check it out! Suchen Sie in Jamals Sätzen auf Seite 76 je einen Relativsatz mit:
1 which **2** that **3** who

B Replace the relative pronoun *that* in these sentences with *who* or *which*.

1 The friend **that** Mia wants to go on holiday with is older than her.
2 The weather **that** they have in Spain in summer is amazing.
3 Jamal and his girlfriend are interested in a kitchen **that** is very expensive.
4 At the moment Tracy has a neighbour **that** drives her to work.

! *on the internet* = im Internet

4 Words, words, words: Money

A Find the verbs in the dialogue on page 76 that match these definitions.

1 plan what you spend every month
2 kept, not spent, your money
3 have money from somebody which you will pay back
4 have enough money to buy something

☆ **Turn to page 99.**

! *to borrow sth* = sich etwas (aus)leihen
to lend sth = etw (ver)leihen

B Complete the sentences with words from the dialogue on page 76.

1 Where do you keep the money you don't spend? – It's in a ___ in the bank. *(2 words)*
2 If we lend you £10,000, can you afford the monthly ___ with your low salary?
3 You need ___ for the car. They will pay if you have an accident.
4 There's nothing wrong with a ___ . Some of them are like a new car. *(2 words)*

☆ **Turn to page 99.**

5 It's your turn

Work with a partner. Talk about your plans. Use these ideas or your own.

▪ saving money ▪ getting advice ▪ spending your money ▪ buying a … ▪ finding a …

EXAMPLE: I'm going to start saving money so I can buy a car.

B Dealing with money

Many everyday conversations are about money.

Video 8

Watch the video and look at page 88 for more information about basic banking.

1 Before you listen

What are these words about money and banking in German? Check on the internet.

1 to change money
2 currency exchange office
3 exchange rates
4 bill
5 note
6 (small) change
7 application form
8 credit limit
9 to recommend
10 bank transfer
11 expiry date
12 security code

2 Listening

40 **A Listen to these people. Match conversations 1–4 with pictures A–D.**

A

B

C

D

B Listen again. Explain what the numbers mean. Stop the recording after each conversation.

Conversation 1	Conversation 2	Conversation 3	Conversation 4
45 minutes	£50	2 years	1-9-2-8
£200	£20	£2,000	9-9-9
tens and twenties	£30	5 days	24 hours

☆ **Turn to page 99.**

C Match the beginnings (1–6) to the endings (a–f) according to the conversations.

1 The young man is taking his girlfriend
2 The young woman
3 At first the waiter didn't believe that
4 To get a credit card
5 Ms Kelly's new credit card
6 The agent doesn't understand

a Ms Kelly must fill out a form.
b will take about five days.
c to Paris to celebrate his first salary.
d has bought a business suit.
e he had made a mistake with the change.
f the last four digits of the credit card.

D Work with a partner. These money expressions were in the dialogues. What do you think they mean?

1 I haven't got money to burn.
2 Money doesn't grow on trees.

!
Im Englischen wird das Währungssymbol vor die Zahl geschrieben: *£200*

3 Mediation

Ihr/e Freund/in hat einen ersten Arbeitsplatz in einer Großstadt gefunden und macht sich Gedanken über seine/ihre Finanzen. Sie finden diesen Artikel zum Thema und möchten sie/ihn darüber informieren.

Budgeting for Beginners

The 50/30/20 rule

Not interested in writing a detailed budget of your monthly expenses? Don't have the time or patience for financial planning? Try the 50/30/20 budget rule.

- **How do I use it?**

The rule asks you to divide your expenses into three categories: **needs**, **wants** and **savings** or **debts**. First, calculate how much money you can put into each category. Let's say your income is €1,500. Then you will have €750 for your needs, €450 for wants and €300 for savings/debts.
Which expenses go in each category?
Needs are expenses which you have to keep in your budget, such as food and rent.
Wants are things which you choose to spend your money on, but you don't need to live your life. This includes things like eating out, holidays and free-time activities.
Savings/debts means money that you put away for the future or money that you owe.

- **Final thought**

If you don't like detailed budgeting, this may be a simple way for you to keep your finances under control. But it won't be suitable for everyone.

Schreiben Sie einen zusammenhängenden Text auf Deutsch in ganzen Sätzen für Ihr/e Freund/in. Erklären Sie:

- wie die 50/30/20 Methode funktioniert.
- was die Vorteile sind.
- was ein möglicher Nachteil sein könnte.

> **!** You write: de**b**t
> But you say: [det]

4 Discussion: Saving and wasting money

A Think about how you spent your money in the past. What advantages and disadvantages were there in the way you spent your money? Will you change things in the future?

B Discuss and answer these questions with a partner. Make notes.

1 Are you saving to buy something?
2 How do you save money?
3 How could you save more money?
4 What do you think is a waste of money?
5 What do you think is expensive, but not a waste of money?

> Every month I save ...

> If I tried hard, I could save ...

C Talk to another pair. Report your partner's answers to the group.

EXAMPLE:

> Sila is saving to buy ...

C Finding a place to live

In Toronto, Jamal decides to move to the city centre.

> **!** apartment = Canadian English
> flat = British English

1 Reading

41 **Read the advertisement and Jamal's email, then do the tasks below.**

Co-Living Homes Toronto

Co-living is your new way of life! Live, work and play together in open areas or relax away from the crowd in your private bedroom. Homes come fully furnished with all utilities included in your monthly bill.

Furnished ✓ Cleaning ✓ Wi-Fi ✓ Streaming service ✓ Laundry ✓ Gym ✓ No extra bills ✓

Hi Mia and Tracy,

Do you remember how tired I was of living so far from the city centre? It always took an hour to get to work or to the good shops. But the normal rents in the city centre were way outside my budget. Well, I've discovered how to live in the centre with a rent that I can afford. It's called 'co-living'. Maybe you've heard of it? In co-living apartments you have your own bedroom, but there's a shared kitchen and work area. The rent you pay every month covers the cost of cleaning, electricity, the internet – everything! There's often a gym in the building which you can use too. So, I've rented a room in an apartment in a part of Toronto where lots of young people live, and last weekend I moved in! I'm feeling really at home after only a week. The people I'm sharing with are friendly and they have interesting jobs. The apartment is on the sixth floor and my room is large and light. (I'll send you some photos later.) The shops, the market and the cafés are all just a few minutes away now. Sometimes it's a bit noisy late at night, but I'm sure I'll get used to that. And anyway, I'm not planning to stay here forever.

Didn't you say you want to move to Manchester, Tracy? Why not try co-living too?

I'll show you the view from my window when we talk on Sunday.

Bye for now,

Jamal

A What is the big news that Jamal wants to share with his friends?

B Use the advertisement and Jamal's email to make notes about the following:

1 costs that are included with the rent in a co-living home
2 how a co-living apartment is different to a regular apartment
3 why Jamal wanted to move
4 the apartment Jamal has moved into
5 a possible problem and Jamal's feelings about it

☆ **Turn to page 100.**

C Discuss your notes with a partner. Would you like a room in a co-living home? Why (not)?

2 Co-living reviews

The last sentence is missing from these reviews about co-living accommodation. Match sentences A–E with 1–4 in the texts. There is one more sentence than you need.

A The managers are just never there. ■ **B** I spend most of my time in the shared rooms.
C I realized I'd made a big mistake. ■ **D** The managers are extremely nice and always helpful.
E There was a real sense of family.

Ari B.	Mel S.	Paul F.	Nikki M.
A great experience! I moved here from Australia and soon felt at home. The people I met taught me so many new things. It was SO much fun! (1)	I have lived here for a few months. It could be a great place if the management was better. They don't repair broken things or check what the cleaners do. (2)	I did a virtual tour and decided that living with so many people wasn't for me. Then I was lonely. I went to check it out and everyone was close, but it was too late. (3)	+: People are really nice. Everyone is single and has a job. -: My room is very small. I always hit my head on something. There could be more room in the shower! (4)

3 Words, words, words: Renting a flat

A Match the words (1–7) with their definitions (a–f).

1	landlord	a	with (or without) furniture
2	(un)furnished	b	money the owner asks for to pay for any damage
3	contract	c	person who you share a flat with
4	deposit	d	owner of the flat which you rent
5	utilities	e	extra things you pay for, e.g. water, electricity, internet
6	roommate	f	agreement in writing with the owner

B Write a sentence with each of these words:

1 balcony 2 parking space 3 lift

4 Discussion

A Work in a small group. Imagine you are looking for a flat to rent. How important are these things? Make two lists: 'must have' and 'would be nice'.

near shops ■ no traffic noise ■ old/modern building ■ balcony ■ parking space ■ light
quiet neighbours ■ furnished/unfurnished ■ public transport ■ modern kitchen ■ lift

B Present your ideas to the group. Agree and disagree with the others' ideas.

EXAMPLE:

One thing that I must have is ...

Really? I couldn't live without ...

Yes, I agree. I'm the same as you.

Skills practice: Brainstorming

Brainstorming ist eine einfache und natürliche Aktivität, die beim Studium oder bei der Arbeit nützlich sein kann. Brainstorming findet häufig in einer Gruppe statt, aber die Techniken lassen sich auch als Einzelperson anwenden.

Get it right: *Tipps für ein erfolgreiches Brainstorming*

- Es gibt verschiedene Brainstorming-Methoden. Die Methoden helfen Ihnen dabei neue Ideen, alleine oder auch gemeinsam in einer Gruppe ausarbeiten.
- Seien Sie für Ideen von den anderen in der Gruppe offen, sowohl für gute als auch für scheinbar schlechte. ‚Schlechte' Ideen zu formulieren sind Teil des Brainstorming-Prozesses.
- Kritisieren Sie die Ideen von anderen nicht – aus vermeintlich unbrauchbaren Einfällen können sich beim Diskutieren in der Gruppe gute Ideen entwickeln
- Jemanden sollte Protokollant / Protokollantin sein und die Ideen schriftlich festhalten. Er/Sie sollte auch die Gruppe beim Thema halten und gut lesbar schreiben können!
- Legen Sie eine Zeit fest. Brainstorming, das eine Stunde übersteigt, ist nicht mehr produktiv.
- In der Schlussphase teilen Sie die Ideen in Kategorien oder Gruppen auf. Dann reduzieren Sie die Zahl, damit am Ende nur die besten übrigbleiben.

A Using a mind map to brainstorm on your own

a) You want to live closer to your work. There are lots of decisions to make before you start looking. Copy the mind map onto a sheet of paper and find places for the words in the box. Add more things you need to think about when looking for somewhere new to live.

buy ▪ cost ▪ house ▪ share with friend

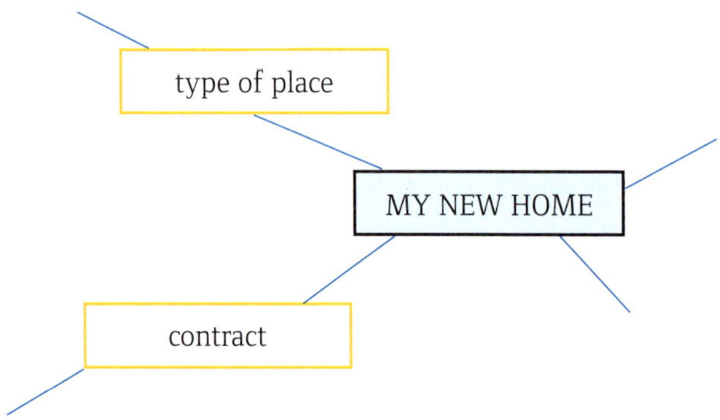

b) Rate the things on your mind map. Give 1 to the things that are most important, 2 to things that would be nice but aren't a must, and 3 to things that you don't really need in your first home.

c) Compare your mind map with a partner. Could you live together in the same co-living apartment? Say why (not).

B Brainstorming with a time limit

a) Work with a partner. You have the chance to work in another country, but you aren't sure if you want to take the job. Copy the table and write down reasons for and against taking the job. They don't all have to be to do with the job. You have five minutes.

For taking the job	Against taking the job
Learn another language	…
…	

b) Compare your list with another pair. What did you all decide to do?

C Brainstorming using questions

a) Work in a small group. Read the situation below and write down a list of questions you need to answer before you make a decision. Begin your questions with *who, what, where, how* and *why*.

> Your boss asks you to join a new working group that is exploring ways to make your company more environmentally friendly. If you agree, you will have more meetings, i.e. more organization, planning and minutes and perhaps more overtime or weekend work. You need to tell your boss tomorrow whether you want to take part.

EXAMPLE: *How much time will I need for the new working group?*

b) Discuss the situation in your group using your questions. Make a decision together.

D Brainstorming thoughts in a grid

Work in a small group. Copy the chart about life in the future. Discuss whether the changes will or won't happen. Tick the boxes. Then think of more possible changes in the future and add them to the grid. Think about your free-time activities, where you might live or work, education, healthcare, …

The world in 2035				
	definitely	possibly	probably not	definitely not
Most cars will be electric.				
Most people will work from home.				
People will go on trips into space.				
…				

E The best brainstorming method

Think about the different brainstorming methods you have tried out. Think about situations where you need to collect ideas. Is one method better than the rest? Why (not)? Discuss in class.

Project page: A personal budget

Work with a partner. You are going to work out a monthly budget for your first salary.

A Read the information about your situation:

- Your net salary is €1,300 a month.
- You are going to move to a small flat, which you will share with a friend.
- You plan to buy a second-hand car to drive to work (10 km away). You have saved €2,000 for this. You need to borrow the rest of the money you need from the bank.

B Talk about …

- the type of flat you should look for and the rent.
- the type of car you should buy and the price.

C Make a budget.

- Copy the form below.
- Which expenses will you share 50:50 with your friend?
- Find out the average cost of things online.
- Agree on amounts to write in the € column.

Monthly expenses	€
Rent	
Utilities (heating, electricity, internet, etc.)	
Mobile phone	
Food	
Travel	
Car payments	
Car expenses (petrol, insurance, etc.)	
Free-time activities / Hobbies	
Eating out	
Savings	
Total expenses	
Total income	

L

Discussing money

- I checked the average cost of …
- It would cost €… to run a small car.
- The estimated price is …
- The rents are about € … for a … square metre flat.
- That's too much / too expensive.
- He could live without …
- She could save a lot if she …
- How much would he spend on … every month?
- How much of her income is for …?
- To borrow €… it would cost €… a month.

D Present your budget to the class and answer their questions. Give the others feedback. Look at page 100 for some useful feedback phrases.

Snapshot

What was your favourite thing in this unit?

What important thing did you learn?

What do you need to work on?

Video tasks

1

1 How to find the right internship

A While you watch

Write down two reasons from Box A why an internship is a good idea and one thing from Box B that you should NOT do to find an internship.

Box A	Box B
a earn some money	**e** Make your CV interesting.
b find out about an industry	**f** Ask family and friends.
c find out if a career is right for you	**g** Start looking when you leave college.
d meet new people	**h** Start to look early.

B What can you remember?

True or false? Correct the false statements.

1. Some people worry that they can't change their career later if they don't like it.
2. There are a number of ways you can make your CV more interesting.
3. Part-time jobs are only useful if you need pocket money.
4. Companies aren't interested in what you learn online.
5. The size of the company where you find an internship doesn't really matter.
6. Don't stop applying for more internships if one application isn't successful.

2

2 How to choose the right career

A While you watch

Copy the diagram and label parts A, B, C and D.

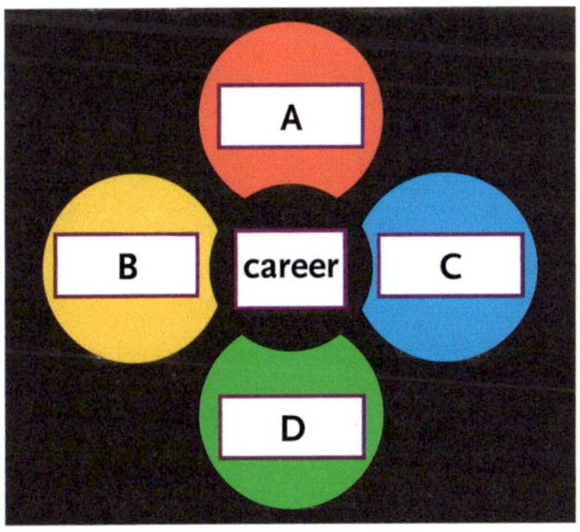

B What can you remember?

Match these things from the video with the right part of the diagram.

1. Love or money?
2. I love travelling and seeing new places.
3. Do you prefer to be in a group or alone?
4. I can explain technical things in simple language.
5. I hate repairing things!
6. I can write computer code.

Video tasks

3

3 How to do a video job interview

A While you watch

Copy the list of tips for a video interview. Number them 1-7 in the order which you see them in the video.

- What the interviewer should see
- How to sit
- What to check before
- Where to have the interview
- How to dress
- How to speak
- When to log in

B What can you remember?

Think about your interview preparations and look at these photos. Write a sentence for each photo in German about your preparations.

4

4 First day at work: do's and don'ts

A While you watch

Match the do's and don'ts with the photos. There are two things which don't match.

Don't arrive late. ■ Don't keep your manager waiting. ■ Don't always be serious.
Don't eat lunch alone. ■ Wear smart clothes. ■ Be friendly.
Ask lots of questions. ■ Prepare answers to questions.

B What can you remember?

1. **Why is it good to eat lunch with your colleagues?**
2. **What could you say to your manager when you leave at the end of your first day?**

5

5 How to reduce plastic at work

A While you watch

Number the photos from 1 to 6 in the order you see them in the video. Then give each photo a title from the box. There are two more titles than you need.

A good speaker ▪ Creative solutions ▪ Filtered tap water ▪ Reusable and washable
Supplier packaging ▪ Team building ▪ The boss ▪ Zero plastic waste

____

____

____

____

____

____

B What can you remember?

Match the sentence beginnings (1–6) with the correct endings (a–f).

1 If there is filtered tap water,
2 A good speaker can inspire staff
3 Use glass bottles and paper cups
4 If you advertise your success,
5 Give everyone a present of
6 Make suppliers use

a to think about the problem of plastic.
b other companies may follow your example.
c staff may stop buying bottled water.
d a personal, reusable water bottle.
e less plastic packaging.
f in the cafeteria.

6

6 How to handle customer complaints

A While you watch

Answer the questions about what the people say.

1 "This is cold. How can I eat it?"– Where is the customer?
2 "Did you repair it? There's still a loud noise."– What is the customer talking about?
3 "I sent five emails and called ten times."– Who is she talking to?
4 "I see. Tell me more."– Who is talking?

B What can you remember?

Match the sentence beginnings (1–4) with the correct endings (a–d).

1 Show the customer
2 If you promise something
3 Always follow up
4 Before you can help

a you understand the problem.
b the customer, you need to ask for the facts.
c that you can't do, you will make the problem worse.
d with a call or an email a few days later.

Video tasks

7 Canada and the Northwest Territories

7

A While you watch

Make a list of the Canadian animals in the box which you see in the video.

Arctic fox ▪ brown bear ▪ buffalo ▪ caribou ▪ eagle ▪ husky dogs
muskox ▪ polar bear ▪ reindeer

B What can you remember?

Are you ready for a trip to Canada and the Northwest Territories? Choose the best answer (a, b or c) to these questions.

1 Canada is the ... country in the world.
a largest **b** second largest **c** third largest

2 Most people live in ...
a in the north. **b** in Toronto and Vancouver. **c** near the border.

3 The Northwest Territories ...
a are three times the size of Germany. **b** are 82 million km^2. **c** have 14 glaciers.

4 Part of the Dempster Highway is ...
a for transporting buffalos. **b** inside the Artic Circle. **c** an ice road.

5 The Territories a fantastic place for the Northern Lights because ...
a of the clear nights and flat landscape. **b** there are lots of hotels. **c** you see them all year.

8 Banking for beginners

8

A While you watch

Copy the table and put the sentences in the right list.

Deposit some money. ▪ Get a statement. ▪ Check the fees. ▪ Show your ID.
Pay with a debit card. ▪ Find where the bank branches are.

Opening a bank account		
Before	**When**	**After**
•	•	•

B What can you remember?

Match the sentence beginnings (1–6) with the endings (a–f).

1 You earn interest on
2 Banks charge fees
3 You deposit money
4 You can get cash from ATMs
5 You can check your account
6 The statement shows you

a what has happened on your account.
b the money in your savings account.
c on your monthly bank statement.
d for their service.
e with your debit card.
f in your account.

Pairwork files

File 1 Unit 1, Part C, Exercise 4B

Partner A: Read the profile below and look at the holiday alternatives on page 11. Talk to partner B and agree where to go on holiday.

You have some money, but not enough to pay for a complete holiday in the UK. You would prefer a full-time job, but you are also happy to work less and have some free time to enjoy the UK. You are a strong swimmer.

File 2 Unit 2, Part B, Exercise 4

Read parts a–j. Agree with partner B on the missing part for each gap in the email.

a the chance to show you this.
b can be available day and night
c completing my third course in game design.
d as advertised on your website (xgaming.com).
e flexible in my hours of work and
f fully meet your requirements.
g I am an ideal candidate for the position
h I attach my CV with full
i often require large teams.
j but I already have more than five years' experience in the gaming world.

File 3 Unit 5, Skills practice, Exercise Ba)

Partner A: Describe the graph to partner B.

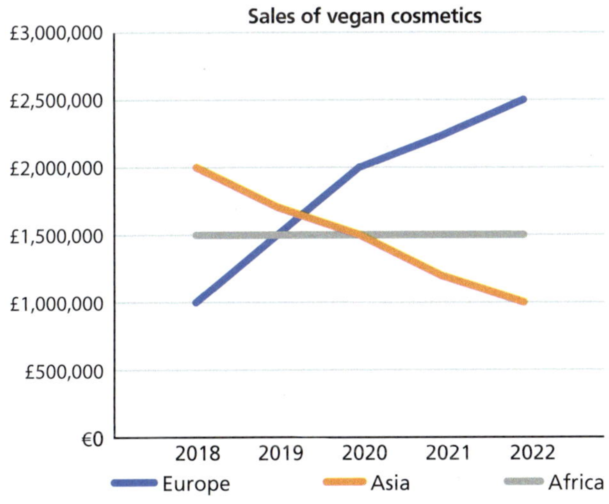

File 4 Unit 2, Part C, Exercise 1

Partner B

Personal information

Name	Tracy Black	Telephone	0772 51298
Address	20 Cotton Lane, Liverpool, L1 0AB	Email	t.black@xxx.nex
Nationality	British		

Professional summary
A highly motivated individual who recently finished college with excellent grades in all subjects. I am looking for an apprenticeship in the IT industry where I can develop my interest in technical support.

Work experience

Sept 202_ - present	**IT Repairs Ltd., Liverpool** Responsibilities: Repairing computers, installing new software
June 201_ - Sept 202_	**Harbour Café, Liverpool** (part-time) Responsibilities: Serving customers and clearing tables
Aug 202_	**Toone Farm, Cornwall** Working holiday

Education and Training

Sept 202_ – June 202_	**Mersey Further Education College, Liverpool** Diploma in Digital and Computing Technologies, Level 2
Sept 201_ – June 202_	**Bishop School, Liverpool** 8 GCSEs with grades A-C in English, Maths and Science

Key skills

Familiar with latest IT and software	Customer service experience
Good at solving technical problems	Good communication skills

Hobbies and interests

Repairing old cars	Sport and fitness

References available on request

File 5 Unit 2, Part C, Exercise 4

Partner B: Ask partner A these questions about where to write the things on your CV.

1 I have finished my apprenticeship in business and management. Where does that go?
2 I speak German, but is it important to say I speak a little Spanish?
3 How about my grades from school? Where do they go?
4 At school I worked as a waiter at weekends for two years. Where should I write that?
5 I had a lot of experience with difficult customers?
6 Where do I write something about the job I'm looking for?
7 Where do I put my email address?

File 6 Unit 3, Skills practice, Exercise A, part a)

Partner B: Look at the participant's calendars. When have they all got time for the meeting?

Elena	Stefan	Richard
Mon: meeting a.m.	Mon: meeting a.m.	Mon: meeting a.m.
Tues:	Tues: meeting a.m.	Tues: holiday
Wed: meeting a.m.	Wed:	Wed:
Thurs: holiday	Thurs:	Thurs: meeting p.m.
Fri:	Fri: meeting p.m.	Fri: meeting p.m.

EXAMPLE:

A: Is Elena busy on Monday morning?

B: Yes, she is. What about Paola? Is she busy then, too?

File 7 Unit 5, Part C, Exercise 3A

Partner B: Answer questions 9–16 below yourself, then ask partner A questions 9–16. Now answer partner A's questions 1–8.
Points for answers: a = 1 point, b = 2 points, c = 3 points.
What's your score? The higher your score the eco-friendlier you are.

9 Your dishwasher is only half full. Do you
- **a** … use the 'quick wash' programme?
- **b** … switch on the normal programme?
- **c** … wait until the dishwasher is full?

10 How do you carry your shopping if you haven't got a bag?
- **a** Buy a plastic bag.
- **b** Buy a green bag.
- **c** It's not that much. I don't need a bag.

11 Do you use a reusable water bottle?
- **a** No, I hate using them.
- **b** Yes, I try to use it, but I often forget.
- **c** Yes, I use it every day.

12 Do you have a washing machine or fridge, etc. that is over 10 years old?
- **a** Yes, I love old things.
- **b** Some are old, and some are new.
- **c** Everything has an energy label A.

13 What type of consumer are you?
- **a** You love shopping.
- **b** When you buy something, it has to be high-quality.
- **c** You only buy what you need.

14 Do you use LED bulbs?
- **a** No, they are expensive.
- **b** We have two, in rooms we use a lot.
- **c** Yes, we only have LED bulbs.

15 Do you give friends eco-friendly tips?
- **a** No, that's boring.
- **b** Yes, but only if they ask.
- **c** Yes, often.

16 When people say 'global warming', do you say:
- **a** I like it to be a bit warmer.
- **b** I read about it, but what can I do?
- **c** Let's do something about it!

File 8 Unit 5, Skills practice, Exercise Ba)

Partner B: Describe the graph to partner A.

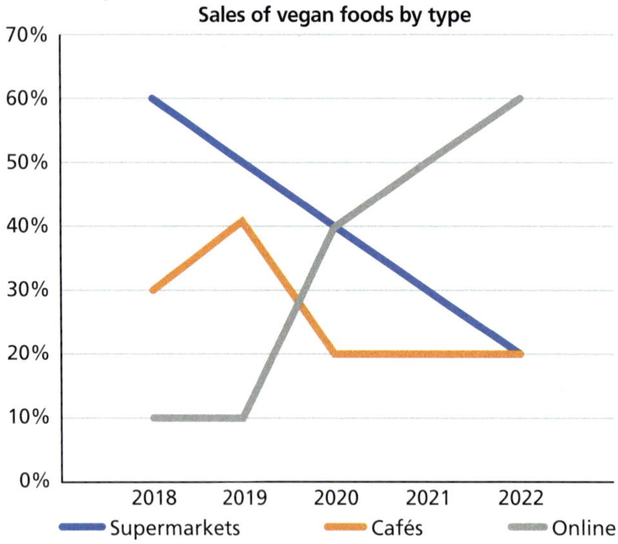

File 9 Unit 7, Part B, Exercise 5

Partner B: Read your role card and be prepared to answer a call from a guest.

Partner B role card

Sie sind am Empfang in des Queen's Hotel. Nachdem ein Gast ausgecheckt hat, ruft er/sie an, weil er/sie seine/ihre Sonnenbrille im Zimmer vergessen hat. Sie nehmen das Telefonat entgegen und fragen folgendes:

- seinen/ihren Namen und seine/ihre Anschrift
- wann sein/ihr Aufenthalt im Hotel war sowie seine/ihre Zimmernummer
- eine Beschreibung der Sonnenbrille
- eine Vermutung, wo er/sie sie vergessen hat

Sagen Sie dem Gast, er/sie soll kurz warten, während Sie mit dem Hauswirtschafter sprechen. Sagen Sie Ihrem Gast, dass die Brille gefunden wurde und fragen Sie, was mit der Brille geschehen soll. Das Hotel kann sie zuschicken, Standardporto übernimmt das Hotel, aber die Expresskosten von €20 müsste der Gast übernehmen.

File 10 Unit 1, Part C, Exercise 4B

Partner B: Read the profile below and look at the holiday alternatives on page 11 of your book. Talk to partner A and agree where to go on holiday.

Your parents have given you some money, so you would prefer to relax and have a holiday in the UK. You love beaches and swimming, but most of all you like exploring new cities.

Differentiation files

Unit 1, Part A, Exercise 2B

☆ **Match the sentence endings to the beginnings.**

1 Yesterday Tracy
2 During his internship, Jamal worked in
3 Mia teaches the refugees German and

a helps them to fill in forms.
b had an interview for a Saturday job.
c four different departments.

★ **Write a second sentence to follow each sentence in your book.**

Unit 1, Part B, Exercise 3A

☆ **Find the English words in the box for the German ones.**

apprenticeship ▪ certificate ▪ exam results ▪ fail ▪ highly qualified ▪ pass
intern ▪ train as ▪ vocational college

1 Praktikant
2 hochqualifiziert
3 Berufsschule
4 Ausbildung
5 Zeugnis
6 Prüfungsergebnisse
7 (eine Prüfung) bestehen
8 (bei einer Prüfung) durchfallen
9 eine Ausbildung zum ... machen

★ **Find the English meanings of these German words. Use a dictionary.**

1 Lehre
2 (Schul)bildung
3 Schulabschlusszeugnis

Unit 1, Part C, Exercise 1B

☆ **Schreiben Sie für die Website der Schule einen zusammenhängenden Text auf Deutsch über Bills Erfahrungen. Verwenden Sie dieses Muster für Ihren Text. Entnehmen Sie dem Text auf Seite 10 alle Informationen, die Sie benötigen.**

Bill Hearn hat der Gruppe erzählt, …
Vor allem bei der Berufswahl sollte man …
Den Umgang mit Geld muss man lernen. Bill z. B. hat Geld verloren, weil …
Wenn Bewerbungen nicht erfolgreich sind, hat Bill den Schülern empfohlen …
Über das Thema Bildung meinte Bill, dass …

★ **Welche von den Sachen, die Bill beschreibt, sind für Sie wichtig und welche sind weniger wichtig? Machen Sie Notizen und erzählen Sie Ihr/e Partner/in darüber.**

Unit 2, Part A, Exercise 3B

☆ **Listen again and complete the sentences with the missing word.**

tasks ▪ taught ▪ works ▪ helped

1 Aiya's brother works in IT and he ___ her a lot.
2 At the start everybody knew Aiya was an apprentice, so they ___ her.
3 Aiya always asked questions and never said 'no' to ___ .
4 Aiya ___ in a team of ten people.

★ **Listen again and complete the sentences.**

1 Aiya ___ for an IT apprenticeship but college sent her ___ .
2 There were ___ candidates for the job, but Aiya ___ for the interview.
3 If Aiya ___ about something, she ___ and asked questions.
4 Aiya ___ her apprenticeship and has a ___ at the bank.

Unit 2, Part B, Exercise 2B

☆ **Which five things does Jamal write about in his covering letter?**

1 die Stelle, auf die er sich bewirbt
2 sein Wunschgehalt
3 die Kenntnisse, die er für die Stelle hat
4 Erfahrungen, die ihm fehlen
5 die Unterlagen im Anhang
6 weshalb er sich auf die Stelle beworben hat
7 wie er von der Stelle erfahren hat
8 eine Aufstellung seiner Zeugnisse und Abschlüsse

★ **Put the things you need in a covering letter in the right order.**

1 the job you are applying for
2 the skills you have for the job
3 the documents you are enclosing
4 any further questions you have
5 why you are applying for the job
6 where you read about the job

Unit 2, Part C, Exercise 1

☆ **Welche drei Aussagen sind falsch?**

1 Im englischen Lebenslauf sind Referenzen verfügbar.
2 Beide Lebensläufe enthalten eine kurze Beschreibung des Bewerbers / der Bewerberin.
3 Ein Foto des Bewerbers / der Bewerberin wird nur in einem der beiden Lebensläufe eingefügt.
4 Alle Zeiträume stehen im englischen Lebenslauf links.
5 Noten und Qualifikationen werden in beiden Lebensläufen angegeben.

★ **Look at the two CVs again and find the following:**

1 a further difference between the two CVs
2 something that is the same in both CVs

Unit 3, Part A, Exercise 3B

☆ **Decide which word is correct in the sentences.**

1 The new assistant wore some strange / strangely shoes yesterday.
2 One member of my team speaks quite aggressive / aggressively.
3 Watch his body language. It's easy / easily to guess what he's thinking.
4 I spoke to her on the phone, but I couldn't understand her very good / well.
5 He learned how to do the job fast / fastly and is very popular.
6 After such a long meeting, I need to find a quiet / quietly place to work.

★ **Complete the sentences with words from the box. Put them in the correct form.**

strong ▪ careful ▪ loud ▪ different

1 I choose the clothes I wear to work ___ .
2 The woman spoke ___ on the phone, but I couldn't understand her.
3 Kevin always starts ___ conversations at the same time.
4 Lin has a ___ voice, she is a good presenter.

Unit 3, Part B, Exercise 4B

☆ **Complete the interviewer's questions with the correct form: a or b.**

1 Why did you decide ___ for this job? **a** to apply **b** applying
2 Do you miss ___ in your home country? **a** to live **b** living
3 Do you mind ___ at weekends? **a** to travel **b** travelling
4 Do you remember ___ those skills? **a** to learn **b** learning
5 Where do you plan ___ in five years? **a** to be **b** being
6 When did you learn ___ Spanish? **a** to speak **b** speaking

★ **Imagine you are the interviewee. Answer the interviewer's questions.**

Unit 3, Part C, Exercise 2

☆ **Listen to the comments about the information on the forum. Which headline (a–e) matches each comment (1–5)?**

a Contact the writer
b Training in small talk
c Culture much more important
d Prefers a quiet life
e Small talk better than arguments

1 I need to train myself to make small talk.
2 What about news and culture?
3 I'm a quiet, private person.
4 Perhaps we could write something together?
5 Lots of conversations end in bad arguments.

★ **Complete the sentences with what the speakers said.**

1 I'm looking for topics which I ___ small talk.
2 ___ important things to talk about.
3 I'm just ___ about sport or the weather.
4 Do you mind me using ___ ?
5 ___ the real world sometimes and have a few moments of peace?

Unit 4, Part A, Exercise 3B

☆ **Read about Tracy's first week. It's Wednesday morning. What has she done? What hasn't she done? Choose the right parts to complete the sentences.**

1 Tracy didn't read / hasn't read the history of Vegan Snacks yet. (*do: Friday*)
2 She has signed / hasn't signed her contract in HR. (*do: Monday*)
3 She has test / hasn't tested the Alpha software. (*do: Friday*)
4 She has opened / hasn't opened a company email account. (*do: Monday*)
5 She has installed / hasn't installed the network update. (*do: Wednesday*)
6 She has picked up / hasn't picked up her door entry card. (*do: Monday*)
7 She has read and signed / hasn't read and signed the security rules. (*do: Tuesday*)

★ **Complete Tracy's sentences with the words in brackets. Do you need the simple past or the present perfect?**

1 I ___ the snacks for my welcome party yet. (not order)
2 I ___ the film about health and safety yesterday. (watch)
3 I ___ already ___ for my monthly train ticket. (pay)
4 I ___ a plant for my desk after work on Monday. (buy)
5 I ___ my big boss yet, she is still on holiday. (not meet)
6 I ___ just ___ my first friend at work. (make)

Unit 4, Part B, Exercise 3B

☆ **Complete the *if*-sentences with the correct form of the verbs in brackets.**

1 If you dress smartly, people ___ that you are serious about your job. (know)
2 If you often smile, your colleagues ___ you are friendly. (think)
3 If you always ___ on time for meetings, you will make a good impression. (arrive)
4 If you ___ carefully to your manager, you will learn a lot. (listen)
5 If you help a busy colleague, people ___ you. (notice)
6 If you play computer games at work, you ___ your trial period. (not pass)

★ **Finish the *if*-sentences with your own ideas.**

1 If I'm invited for an interview, …
2 I'll buy a new bag if …
3 If I get the job, …
4 If I work in another town, …
5 I'll make a cake for my welcome party if …
6 You'll come and see my new flat if …

Unit 4, Part C, Exercise 2

☆ **Complete the sentences with the English words for the words in brackets.**

1 Nurses in the hospital do three ___ (*Schichten*). Jill doesn't like to work nights.
2 Sometimes doctors have to ___ (*zur Welt bringen*) babies at night.
3 In the morning I need my password to ___ (*sich einloggen*).
4 When we have an online meeting, we always ___ (*begrüßen*) each other before we look at the agenda.
5 Jack can't repair the old boat if he doesn't have the ___ (*Ersatzteile*).
6 All the goods go to a large ___ (*Lager*) first, then they go to shops or private customers.

★ **Read the text on page 40 again and then complete these sentences.**

1 It was ___ for Jill all morning.
2 In Jill's job, you need to be caring, ___ and skilled.
3 ___ or exercise help Angus start his day.
4 During the day, Angus ___ the dishwasher or does his laundry, too.
5 It's ___ work at the boatyard and Jack is always learning on the job.
6 Everybody who works at the boatyard is ___ and loves boats.

Unit 5, Part A, Exercise 3B

☆ **Complete what the factory workers said at a meeting about plastic. Use *if*-sentences type 2 with the correct form of the verb in brackets.**

1 If we used plastic for 3D printing, we ___ more. (recycle)
2 If Hassan came to the next meeting, he ___ us more details. (give)
3 If we did that, our products ___ more. (cost)
4 If we sorted the plastic into different colours, it ___ easier to recycle. (be)
5 If we made a list of the plastic we use, we ___ a better idea of where to start. (have)
6 If we looked for another type of packaging, I'm sure we ___ one. (find)

Unit 5, Part B, Exercise 4B

☆ **Choose the correct word to complete the notes Tracy made when she listened to the interview.**

1 Marketing eco-friendly products is different

- (1) Consumers / Companies want eco-friendly products.
- But (2) when / how do you find them?

2 Steps in the campaign

Liv's job was to convince customers to (3) listen to her / pay more. How?

- Only (4) 10% / 20% of plastic sunglasses are (5) used / recycled. She gave customers the facts and asked, "What happens if you (6) don't buy / don't wear our glasses?"
- To show that the company is serious about the (7) glasses / environment, we promised:
  … to support Save Our Oceans and (8) promise them 1% / give them 3% of profits.
  … to clean 10 kilos of (9) from beaches / from the ocean for every 10 pairs of glasses sold.

3 Results

- High sales
- (10) 90% / 95% were new customers.

Unit 5, Part C, Exercise 2

☆ **Complete the text with the English for the German words. All the words are in the text on page 50.**

In the 21st century, (1 *Klimawandel*) has made the (2 *Erde*) much warmer. The (3 *Treibhausgas*) which comes from (4 *Mülldeponien*) is part of the problem. These are full of our waste which is not (5 *wiederverwertbar*).
What can we do to take more care of the environment? There are small things. We can, for example, buy electrical (6 *Haushaltsgeräte*) which are (7 *energieeffizient*) with an energy label A. And when we go shopping or get a takeaway, we can take our own (8 *Behälter*).

Unit 6, Part A, Exercise 4

☆ **You went on an English course in Oxford. The description in their brochure was false. Complete the letter of complaint with these sentences.**

a very small classroom ▪ because all the ▪ look forward to ▪ to complain about ▪ it states

I'm writing (1) the language course I booked at your school last month. In the description of the course (2) that lessons only take place in the morning, and afternoons are free for sightseeing. But when I arrived, I found that we there were afternoon lessons three days a week. Your brochure also states that classes have no more than 12 students. There were 18 students in (3). Finally, I choose the course (4) teachers were British native speakers. This was not true. Two of our teachers were from Malaysia.
I (6) hearing from you.

Unit 6, Part B, Exercise 3B

☆ **Complete the sentences with the verbs in brackets. Use the will future.**

1 The child is crying. I ___ with him. (sit)
2 She can't see. I ___ someone to help. (find)
3 They're sad. We ___ do something. (have to)
4 We're late. We ___ the film. (not catch)
5 It is so hot. I ___ the window. (open)
6 That bag is heavy. I ___ you with it. (help)

Unit 6, Part C, Exercise 1C

☆ **Partner A: Read Barbara Uan's text again. Make sentences about the differences between China and Germany. Then read them to partner B.**

1 small dishes • Sven doesn't enjoy • with lots of • meals
2 flat • looked at • Barbara and Sven's • Bai • all the things in
3 don't open • is still there • people • when the guest • presents
4 in China • number • is • a lucky • two

☆ **Partner B: Read Ulrich Clark's text again. Make sentences about things which were new for him in Germany. Then read them to partner A.**

1 start work • early • many Germans
2 and • late for meetings • punctual • they • are • not
3 before • isn't much • a meeting • there • small talk
4 at work • much • don't joke • people

Unit 7, Part A, Exercise 3B

☆ **Complete these sentences with the verbs in brackets and the *going to* future.**

1 Jamal, Tracy and Mia ___ to the CN Tower. (go)
2 Tracy ___ as long as Mia in Canada. (not stay)
3 Mia ___ more than 2,000 miles on the train. (travel)
4 ___ Jamal ___ Mia and Tracy to his uncle? (introduce)
5 Mia ___ Montreal. (not visit)
6 ___ you ___ us your office, Jamal? (show)

Unit 7, Part B, Exercise 2B

☆ **Match the sentence endings to the beginnings.**

1 Tracy left her tablet
2 Tracy had stayed in
3 Tracy expects to arrive at Lake View
4 She isn't going to see Nuna because

a in less than an hour.
b in the safe.
c she isn't going to be on duty.
d room 2024.

Unit 7, Part B, Exercise 5

Partner A role card

You stayed at the Queen's Hotel and left some sunglasses in your room. Call the hotel from home. Have the following information ready:

- your name and address
- the dates of your stay and your room number
- a description of the sunglasses
- where you left them

Partner B role card

You are a receptionist at the Queen's Hotel. You answer a call from a guest who has left some sunglasses in their room. Ask the guest for:

- their name and address
- a description of the sunglasses
- the dates of their stay and their room number
- where they left the sunglasses

Then ask the guest to hold the line so you can speak to the housekeeper. Tell the guest the housekeeper has found the sunglasses and ask what you should do with them. The hotel will pay the cost of sending them. But if you send them express, it will cost an extra €20.

Unit 7, Part C, Exercise 5A

☆ **Use this model for your description.**

It's about … kilometres from the east/west coast. The land is (flat) and there are a lot of (lakes).
The weather there is … in winter/summer. In this part of Canada people have jobs as …

Unit 8, Part A, Exercise 4A

☆ **Match the verbs with the definitions.**

1 plan what you spend every month
2 kept, not spent, your money
3 have money from somebody which you will pay back
4 have enough money to buy something

a saved
b afford
c budget
d borrow

Unit 8, Part A, Exercise 4B

☆ **Complete the sentences with the English words for the words in brackets. All the words are in the dialogue on page 76.**

1 Where do you keep the money you don't spend? – It's in a ___ in the bank. *(Sparkonto)*
2 If we lend you £10,000, can you afford the monthly ___ with your low salary? *(Raten)*
3 You need ___ for the car. They will pay if you have an accident. *(eine Versicherung)*
4 There's nothing wrong with a ___. Some of them are like a new car. *(Gebrauchtwagen)*

Unit 8, Part B, Exercise 2B

☆ **Listen again. Complete the sentences.**

Conversation 1
Their plane ___ in 45 minutes.
They want to ___ £200 into euros.
They want the money in €10 and €20 ___.

Conversation 2
The woman gave the ___ a £50 note.
He only gave her ___ for £20.
The ___ of her change is £30.

Conversation 3
She has had an account with the bank for two ___.
The ___ limit will be £2000.
The credit card will take about five ___ days to arrive.

Conversation 4
1-9-2-8 are the last four ___ of the credit card number.
9-9-9 is the ___ code.
An email with the tickets will arrive in the next 24 ___.

Unit 8, Part C, Exercise 1B

☆ **Complete the sentences with one word in each gap.**

1 The monthly rent in a co-living apartment covers all the ___ .
2 In a co-living apartment, you have your own ___ but you share a ___ and a work area.
3 Jamal didn't want to live so ___ from the city centre.
4 The people Jamal lives with are ___ and he has a ___ room.
5 Jamal believes he will get used to the ___ at night.

Useful feedback phrases

It isn't always easy to give people feedback. It is easy to be negative or positive, but not so easy to give useful advice. It is good if you say something negative, to give an example of how you think the person could make it better.

L

Giving feedback		
😊	😐	☹
▪ The design is very clear. ▪ The … covers everything. ▪ I liked your … because … ▪ Smile, you don't then look so nervous. ▪ The … is well-structured. ▪ It was easy to find the information I needed. ▪ There isn't too much information on the … ▪ There are no spelling mistakes. ▪ You could answer all our questions really well. ▪ My favourite part is … because …	▪ The structure is clear. ▪ I would add … to the list. ▪ I think … would be better. ▪ I think your … would be better if you … ▪ Less information would have made it easier to read. ▪ Fewer photos would have been better. ▪ You knew quite a lot about the topic, but you couldn't answer our questions clearly.	▪ Sorry, but it looks a bit messy. ▪ There are some important things missing in the list. ▪ You forgot to include … ▪ I didn't like your ... because … ▪ Your … wasn't very clear. ▪ I couldn't find the information I needed. ▪ There was too much information on the … ▪ Check your text next time, there were a few mistakes in it. ▪ You need to find out more about the topic than the information you tell us so you can answer any questions better. ▪ My least favourite part is … because …

Don't forget to thank people for their feedback.

Chronologische Wortliste

Wörter aus dem Band Do it! A1/A2 werden in dieser Liste als bekannt vorausgesetzt.
Wörter aus den Audiotexten sind mit einem gelben Balken und Wörter aus den Pairwork files mit einem türkisenen Balken gekennzeichnet.

AE = American English | *n* = noun *(Substantiv)* | *adj* = adjective | <> = opposite *(Gegensatz)*
BE = British English | *v* = verb | *pl* = plural

UNIT 1

5	**computing**	[kəmˈpjuːtɪŋ]	*n* computer	Datenverarbeitung
	health care	[ˈhelθ keə]	*adj* healthy, unhealthy	Gesundheitswesen, Gesundheitsfürsorge
	social care	[ˌsəʊʃl ˈkeə]	sb who is a nurse works in social care	Sozialwesen, Sozialfürsorge
	horse riding	[ˈhɔːsraɪdɪŋ]	*v* to ride a horse	Reiten
	reception	[rɪˈsepʃn]	the place in a hotel where you check in	Empfang, Rezeption
6	to **keep in touch with sb**	[ˌkiːp ɪn ˈtʌtʃ wɪð]	to keep in contact	mit jdm in Verbindung bleiben
	to **service sth**	[ˈsɜːvɪs]	you get your car serviced at the garage	etw warten, etw instandhalten
	especially	[ɪˈspeʃəli]	particularly	besonders, insbesondere
	by the hour	[baɪ ði ˈaʊə]	e.g. Students are usually paid by the hour.	stundenweise, pro Stunde
	choice	[tʃɔɪs]	*v* to choose	Wahl
	internship	[ˈɪntɜːnʃɪp]	*n* intern	Praktikum
	to **fill in a form**	[fɪl ˌɪn ə ˈfɔːm]	to write your details on a form	ein Formular ausfüllen
	to **translate**	[trænsˈleɪt]	*n* translation	übersetzen
	to **bake**	[beɪk]	to cook a cake	backen
	Take care!	[ˌteɪk ˈkeə]	Look after yourself!	Pass auf dich auf! Mach's gut!
	packaging	[ˈpækɪdʒɪŋ]	*n* package	Verpackung
	to **transport sth**	[trænˈspɔːt]	to move sth from one place to another	etw befördern, etw transportieren
	design	[dɪˈzaɪn]	*v* to design	Konstruktion, Design
	department	[dɪˈpɑːtmənt]	e.g. Companies have lots of different departments.	Abteilung
	sales *pl*	[seɪlz]	*v* to sell	Vertrieb, Verkauf
	human resources (HR) *pl*	[ˌhjuːmən rɪˈsɔːsɪz]	this department is important for employees	Personal(abteilung)
	to **experience sth**	[ɪkˈspɪəriəns]	*n* experience	etw erfahren, etw erleben
	organization	[ˌɔːgənaɪˈzeɪʃn]	*v* to organize	(größeres) Unternehmen
7	**almost**	[ˈɔːlməʊst]	nearly	fast, beinahe
	factory	[ˈfæktəri]	e.g. A lot of things are made in factories.	Fabrik
8	**What's up?**	[ˌwɒts ˈʌp]	What's the matter?	Was gibt's?
	to **train as a …**	[ˈtreɪn əz ə]	*n* trainee	eine Ausbildung zum … machen
	suit	[suːt]	trousers or a skirt and a matching jacket	Anzug
	mentor	[ˈmentɔː]	sb who helps you if you have a problem	Mentor/in
	highly-qualified	[ˌhaɪli ˈkwɒlɪfaɪd]	sb who has lots of qualifications and experience	hochqualifiziert
	to **breathe**	[briːð]	*n* breath	atmen, durchatmen
9	**intern**	[ˈɪntɜːn]	*n* internship	Praktikant/in
	to **learn about sth**	[ˈlɜːn əbaʊt]	e.g. I learned about the company before the interview.	etw über etw in Erfahrung bringen
	to **apply for sth**	[əˈplaɪ fə]	*n* application	sich für/um etw bewerben
	to **imagine sth**	[ɪˈmædʒɪn]	*n* imagination	sich etw vorstellen
	to **be highly likely**	[bi ˌhaɪli ˈlaɪkli]	there is a high chance	sehr wahrscheinlich sein
	to **feel excited about sth**	[ˌfiːl ɪkˈsaɪtɪd əbaʊt]	when you can't wait for sth to happen	von etw begeistert sein
10	to **start a company**	[ˌstɑːt ə ˈkʌmpəni]	to found or begin a company	ein Unternehmen gründen
	to **manage sth**	[ˈmænɪdʒ]	*n* manager	etw verwalten, mit etw umgehen
	overdraft	[ˈəʊvədrɑːft]	*v* to overdraw	Kontoüberziehung, Dispo, Minus
	frustrated	[frʌˈstreɪtɪd]	*n* frustration	frustriert
	education	[ˌedʒuˈkeɪʃn]	*v* to educate	Bildung, Ausbildung, Lernen
	journey	[ˈdʒɜːni]	a journey is usually longer than a trip	Reise, Weg
	to **graduate**	[ˈgrædʒueɪt]	*n* graduation	den (Uni-/Schul-)Abschluss machen

	uneducated	[ʌnˈedʒukeɪtɪd]	<> educated	ungebildet, schlecht ausgebildet
	quote	[kwəʊt]	*v* to quote	Zitat
	present moment	[ˌpreznt ˈməʊmənt]	now	Augenblick
11	**careers advisor**	[kəˈrɪəz ədvaɪzə]	sb who gives you advice about your career	Berufsberater/in
	income	[ˈɪnkʌm]	the money you earn	Einkommen
	satisfaction	[ˌsætɪsˈfækʃn]	*adj* satisfied	Zufriedenheit
	to **register**	[ˈredʒɪstə]	*n* registration	sich anmelden
	greetings *pl*	[ˈgriːtɪŋz]	*v* to greet sb	Grüße
	to **celebrate**	[ˈselɪbreɪt]	*n* celebration	feiern
	to **be up to sth**	[bi ˈʌp tə]	to do sth you probably shouldn't be doing	etw vorhaben, etw machen, etw anstellen
	to **pick fruit**	[ˌpɪk ˈfruːt]	to take the fruit off trees and bushes	Obst pflücken, Obst ernten
	accommodation	[əˌkɒməˈdeɪʃn]	e.g. hotels, hostels, bed and breakfast places	Unterkunft
	a strong swimmer	[ə ˌstrɒŋ ˈswɪmə]	<> a weak swimmer	ein/e gute/r Schwimmer/in
12	**to break the ice**	[ˌbreɪk ði ˈaɪs]	to start a conversation with sb	das Eis brechen
	May I join you?	[ˌmeɪ aɪ ˈdʒɔɪn juː]	May I sit here? May I join this conversation?	Darf ich mich zu Ihnen gesellen/setzen?
13	to **socialize**	[ˈsəʊʃəlaɪz]	to meet other people	sich (privat) mit Leuten treffen
	name tag	[ˈneɪm tæg]	a label you wear with your name on it	Namensschild
	stranger	[ˈstreɪndʒə]	<> friend, sb you know	Fremde/r, Unbekannte/r
	business card	[ˈbɪznəs kɑːd]	e.g. A business card has your name, position and company on it.	(geschäftliche) Visitenkarte
	training course	[ˈtreɪnɪŋ kɔːs]	e.g. When you start a new job there is often a training course.	Schulung
14	to **divide sth into sth**	[dɪˈvaɪd ɪntə]	to share sth between more people or things	etw in etw aufteilen
	to **prepare sth**	[prɪˈpeə]	*n* preparation	etw *(Text usw.)* erstellen
	bar chart	[ˈbɑː tʃɑːt]	used to explain data	Säulendiagramm
	pie chart	[ˈpaɪ tʃɑːt]	a diagram that looks like a pie to explain data	Tortendiagramm
	I have no idea.	[aɪ həv ˌnəʊ aɪˈdɪə]	<> I know.	Ich habe keine Ahnung.
	summer school	[ˈsʌmə skuːl]	courses in holidays to help you be better at sth	Ferienkurs(e)
	design	[dɪˈzaɪn]	*n* designer	Gestaltung, Layout
	to **cover sth**	[ˈkʌvə]	to talk about sth	etw *(Thema usw.)* behandeln
	well-structured	[ˌwel ˈstrʌktʃəd]	<> badly-structured	übersichtlich aufgebaut, gut strukturiert
	structure	[ˈstrʌktʃə]	*v* to structure	Aufbau, Struktur
	messy	[ˈmesi]	<> tidy, clean	chaotisch, unübersichtlich

UNIT 2

15	**application**	[ˌæplɪˈkeɪʃn]	e.g. I sent my application, but I forgot to attach my CV!	Bewerbung
	vocational area	[vəʊˌkeɪʃənl ˈeəriə]	e.g. I can't decide which vocational area is for me.	Berufsfeld
	business training	[ˈbɪznəs treɪnɪŋ]	when you learn all about what happens in a business	kaufmännische Ausbildung
	construction	[kənˈstrʌkʃn]	*v* to construct sth	Baugewerbe
	childcare	[ˈtʃaɪldkeə]	looking after children	Kinderbetreuung
	technical training	[ˈteknɪkl treɪnɪŋ]	when you learn a technical job	technische Ausbildung
	catering	[ˈkeɪtərɪŋ]	e.g. cooking food, serving food, planning food, …	Gastronomie
	applicant	[ˈæplɪkənt]	*v* to apply	Bewerber/in
	leader	[ˈliːdə]	*v* to lead	Führungspersönlichkeit
	organized	[ˈɔːgənaɪzd]	*v* to organize	(gut) organisiert
	firefighter	[ˈfaɪəfaɪtə]	sb who fights fires	Feuerwehrmann/-frau
	captain	[ˈkæptɪn]	e.g. The captain is the boss of a boat or ship.	Kapitän/in
16	**needs** *pl*	[niːdz]	the things you need to live your life	Bedürfnisse
	support	[səˈpɔːt]	*v* to support	Hilfe, Unterstützung
	to **develop sth**	[dɪˈveləp]	*n* development	etw entwickeln
	to **test sth**	[test]	e.g. We tested the brakes and they worked.	etw prüfen, etw testen
	cyber security	[ˌsaɪbə sɪˈkjʊərəti]	e.g. Cyber security is very important today.	Cybersicherheit
	attention to detail	[əˌtenʃn tə ˈdiːteɪl]	e.g. Attention to detail is important in this job.	Detailgenauigkeit, Liebe zum Detail
	to **cause sth**	[kɔːz]	*n* cause	etw verursachen
	to **change**	[tʃeɪndʒ]	*n* change	sich verändern

	to work long hours	[wɜːk ˌlɒŋ ˈaʊəz]	e.g. In some jobs you have to work long hours.	lange arbeiten, Überstunden machen
	to update sth	[ˌʌpˈdeɪt]	*n* update	etw aktualisieren, etw updaten
	network	[ˈnetwɜːk]	e.g. It's useful to have a good network of contacts.	Netzwerk, Netz
	permanent job	[ˌpɜːmənənt ˈdʒɒb]	<> temporary job	unbefristete Stelle, Festanstellung
17	**fun**	[fʌn]	<> boring	lustig, spaßig
	arts and crafts *pl*	[ˌɑːts ənd ˈkrɑːfts]	e.g. The children paint pictures in arts and crafts.	Basteln, Werken
	discovery	[dɪˈskʌvəri]	*v* to discover	Entdeckung
	to behave	[bɪˈheɪv]	*n* behaviour	sich benehmen
	to fall asleep	[ˌfɔːl əˈsliːp]	e.g. I fell asleep in front of the TV last night.	einschlafen
	playground	[ˈpleɪgraʊnd]	the place in a park where children like to play	Spielplatz
	to cycle	[ˈsaɪkl]	to ride a bike	radeln
18	**global leader**	[ˌgləʊbl ˈliːdə]	e.g. Global leaders are often big companies.	Weltmarktführer
	head office	[ˌhed ˈɒfɪs]	e.g. Head offices of companies are usually in cities.	Zentrale, Firmensitz
	to support sb/sth	[səˈpɔːt]	to give sb help	jdn/etw unterstützen
	HR manager	[eɪtʃ ˌɑː ˈmænɪdʒə]	sb who is boss of the HR department	Personalleiter/in, Personalsachbearbeiter/in
	file	[faɪl]	*v* to file	Datei, Aktenordner
	records *pl*	[ˈrekɔːdz]	*v* to record	Datensätze, Akten
	to keep sth up to date	[kiːp ˌʌp tə ˈdeɪt]	e.g. Make sure you keep the information up to date.	etw auf dem neuesten Stand halten
	reference	[ˈrefərəns]	e.g. Your references can help you get a job.	Referenz
	diploma	[dɪˈpləʊmə]	e.g. We get a diploma at the end of the course.	Diplom, Abschlusszeugnis
	business administration	[ˈbɪznəs ədmɪnɪstreɪʃn]	e.g. Business administration is very interesting.	Betriebswirtschaft
	organizational	[ˌɔːgənaɪˈzeɪʃənl]	*n* organization	organisatorisch, Organisations-
	bilingual	[ˌbaɪˈlɪŋgwəl]	to be able to speak two languages	zweisprachig
	to advertise a job	[ˌædvətaɪz ə ˈdʒɒb]	*n* advertisement	eine Stelle ausschreiben
	to package sth	[ˈpækɪdʒ]	*n* package	etw verpacken
	to grow	[grəʊ]	*n* growth	wachsen
	focus (on sth)	[ˈfəʊkəs]	e.g. The main focus is on what you want to learn.	Schwerpunkt (auf etw)
	to qualify	[ˈkwɒlɪfaɪ]	*n* qualification	den/seinen Abschluss machen
	to enclose sth	[ɪnˈkləʊz]	e.g. Don't forget to enclose your CV.	*(Brief:)* etw beifügen
	further	[ˈfɜːðə]	e.g. Don't walk any further along the path.	weiter
19	**salary**	[ˈsæləri]	the money a company pays you	Gehalt
	to be familiar with sth	[bi fəˈmɪliə wɪð]	e.g. I'm familiar with this picture. I've seen it before.	mit etw vertraut sein, sich mit etw auskennen
	coding	[ˈkəʊdɪŋ]	*v* to code	Programmierung
	to meet requirements	[miːt rɪˈkwaɪəmənts]	e.g. You have to meet the requirements for the job.	Voraussetzungen erfüllen
	to attach sth	[əˈtætʃ]	*n* attachment	*(E-Mail:)* etw anhängen
	to require sth	[rɪˈkwaɪə]	*n* requirement	etw erfordern, etw benötigen
20	**recently**	[ˈriːsntli]	*adj* recent	vor kurzem
	repair	[rɪˈpeə]	*v* to repair	Reparatur
	harbour	[ˈhɑːbə]	the place where boats arrive	Hafen
	to clear a table	[ˌklɪər ə ˈteɪbl]	<> to lay the table	den Tisch abräumen
	working holiday	[ˌwɜːkɪŋ ˈhɒlədeɪ]	when you work and have a holiday too	Arbeitsurlaub
	further education	[ˌfɜːðər edʒuˈkeɪʃn]	e.g. A university is further education.	Weiterbildung
	on request	[ɒn rɪˈkwest]	e.g. On request we'll send you a brochure.	auf Anfrage
21	**birdwatching**	[ˈbɜːdwɒtʃɪŋ]	*v* to watch birds	Vogelbeobachtung
	serious	[ˈsɪəriəs]	e.g. She is a serious candidate for the job.	ernstzunehmend
	to be relevant to sth	[bi ˈreləvənt tə]	e.g. Is this information relevant for the job?	einen Bezug zu etw haben, mit etw zu tun haben
	keyword	[ˈkiːwɜːd]	an important word	Stichwort
	key	[kiː]	e.g. This is one of my key arguments.	wichtig, entscheidend, Haupt-
22	**to contact sb**	[ˈkɒntækt]	e.g. Contact me if you have any questions.	sich mit jdm in Verbindung setzen
	to learn sth	[lɜːn]	e.g. I'd like to learn more about the job.	etw erfahren
23	**alternative**	[ɔːlˈtɜːnətɪv]	another possibility	andere/r/s, Ausweich-, alternativ
	action point	[ˈækʃn pɔɪnt]	e.g. I only wrote down the action points.	Maßnahme, Aktionspunkt

	travel expenses *pl*	[ˈtrævl ɪkspensɪz]	the money you spend on travel	Reisekosten
	attachment	[əˈtætʃmənt]	*v* to attach	*(E-Mail:)* Anhang
	medical check-up	[ˌmedɪkl ˈtʃekʌp]	e.g. You need a medical check-up for some jobs.	ärztliche Untersuchung
24	**business assistant**	[ˈbɪznəs əsɪstənt]	e.g. I have a job as a business assistant.	kaufmännische/r Assistent/in
	carpenter	[ˈkɑːpəntə]	sb who works with wood	Schreiner/in, Tischler/in
	landscape gardener	[ˈlændskeɪp gɑːdnə]	sb who works outside in parks and gardens	Landschaftsgärtner/in
	optician	[ɒpˈtɪʃn]	sb who tests people's eyes	Optiker/in
	tattoo artist	[təˈtuː ɑːtɪst]	sb who draws pictures on people's bodies	Tätowierer/in

UNIT 3

25	**professional life**	[prəˌfeʃənl ˈlaɪf]	<> personal life	Berufsleben
	untidy	[ʌnˈtaɪdi]	<> tidy	unaufgeräumt, unordentlich
	to **be a mess**	[bi ə ˈmes]	<> to be tidy	unordentlich sein, schlampig sein
	sb ought to do sth	[ˌɔːt tə ˈduː]	e.g. Somebody ought to tell him he's always late.	jd sollte etw tun
26	to **make an impression**	[meɪk ən ɪmˈpreʃn]	e.g. She made a good first impression at the interview.	einen Eindruck hinterlassen
	neat and tidy	[niːt ən ˈtaɪdi]	<> messy	sauber und ordentlich
	casual	[ˈkæʒuəl]	<> formal	*(Kleidung:)* leger, salopp
	to **sit up straight**	[sɪt ˌʌp ˈstreɪt]	e.g. Some people don't sit up straight when they eat.	gerade sitzen
	brief	[briːf]	<> long	kurz
	dos and don'ts *pl*	[ˌduːz ən ˈdəʊnts]	e.g. Read the list of dos and don'ts.	*Dinge, die man tun bzw. lassen sollte*
	to **take sth seriously**	[teɪk ˈsɪəriəsli]	to be serious about sth	etw ernst nehmen
	greeting	[ˈgriːtɪŋ]	*v* to greet sb	Begrüßung
	to **act**	[ækt]	e.g. He acted correctly in the situation.	handeln
	accordingly	[əˈkɔːdɪŋli]	e.g. She was dressed accordingly.	entsprechend
28	to **mind**	[maɪnd]	to be against sth	etw dagegen haben
	to **look after sth**	[lʊk ˈɑːftə]	to take care of sth	sich um etw kümmern
	link	[lɪŋk]	*v* to link	Bindeglied, Verbindung
	to **have sth lined up**	[həv ˌlaɪnd ˈʌp]	to have sth organized	etw vorhaben, etw geplant haben
29	**Take your time.**	[ˌteɪk jɔː ˈtaɪm]	Don't hurry!	Lassen Sie sich Zeit!
	to **have arguments about sth**	[həv ˈɑːgjumənts əbaʊt]	to disagree about sth	sich um etw streiten
	to **specialize in sth**	[ˈspeʃəlaɪz ɪn]	to focus on sth (and be good at it)	sich auf etw spezialisieren
	health and safety	[ˌhelθ ənd ˈseɪfti]	e.g. Health and safety are important at work.	Arbeitssicherheit
	to **make sense**	[ˌmeɪk ˈsens]	to be a good idea	einleuchten, vernünftig sein
	contract	[ˈkɒntrækt]	e.g. Don't work without a contract.	Vertrag
	starting salary	[ˈstɑːtɪŋ sæləri]	the money you get when you start a job	Einstiegsgehalt, Anfangsgehalt
	truth	[truːθ]	<> lies	Wahrheit
30	**silence**	[ˈsaɪləns]	<> loudness	Stille
	blood	[blʌd]	e.g. There was a lot of blood after the accident.	Blut
	private person	[ˌpraɪvət ˈpɜːsn]	<> outgoing person	zurückhaltender Mensch
	culture	[ˈkʌltʃə]	e.g. Different countries have different cultures.	Kultur
	peace	[piːs]	*adj* peaceful	Frieden
31	to **keep sth going**	[kiːp ˈgəʊɪŋ]	e.g. It was hard to keep the conversation going.	etw am Laufen halten
	Go ahead.	[ˌgəʊ əˈhed]	Tell me about it! You start!	Schieß los! Erzähl mal!
	amazing	[əˈmeɪzɪŋ]	<> boring, uninteresting	toll, unglaublich
	incredible	[ɪnˈkredəbl]	e.g. It was an incredible story the man told.	unglaublich
	seriously	[ˈsɪəriəsli]	e.g. She takes everything seriously.	im Ernst
	I never guessed.	[aɪ ˌnevə ˈgest]	I wouldn't have thought that.	Das hätte ich nie gedacht. Darauf wäre ich nie gekommen.
	festival	[ˈfestɪvl]	e.g. Different cultures have different festivals.	Fest, Festtag
	to **throw sth at sb**	[θrəʊ]	<> to catch sth	jdn mit etw bewerfen
	coloured	[ˈkʌləd]	<> plain, non-coloured	farbig, bunt
	powder	[ˈpaʊdə]	e.g. We all threw coloured powder.	Pulver
	to **change one's clothes**	[ˌtʃeɪndʒ wʌnz ˈkləʊðz]	e.g. We changed our clothes because they were dirty.	sich umziehen

	never in a million years	[ˌnevər ɪn ə ˌmɪljən ˈjɪəz]	e.g. I never in a million years thought you'd come.	nie im Leben
	to **shout at sb**	[ˈʃaʊt ət]	*n* shout	jdn anschreien
32	**participant**	[pɑːˈtɪsɪpənt]	*v* to participate	Teilnehmer/in
	agenda	[əˈdʒendə]	sth you send to everyone attending a meeting	Tagesordnung
33	to **rewrite sth**	[ˌriːˈraɪt]	e.g. I had to rewrite my report for the boss.	etw umformulieren, etw neu schreiben
	biscuit	[ˈbɪskɪt]	e.g. Americans say cookies not biscuits.	Keks
	conclusions *pl*	[kənˈkluːʒnz]	*v* to conclude	Fazit
34	**scriptwriter**	[ˈskrɪptraɪtə]	sb who writes scripts for films and plays	Drehbuchautor/in
	camera operator	[ˌkæmərə ˈɒpəreɪtə]	sb who operates a (film) camera	Kameramann/-frau

UNIT 4

35	**receptionist**	[rɪˈsepʃənɪst]	sb who works at the reception	Empfangsmitarbeiter/in, Rezeptionist/in
	flight attendant	[ˌflaɪt əˈtendənt]	sb who works on a plane	Flugbegleiter/in
	immigration officer	[ˌɪmɪˈgreɪʃn ɒfɪsə]	sb who checks people's passports at an airport	Grenzbeamte/r, Beamte/r bei der Einreisekontrolle
	customer service agent	[ˌkʌstəmə sɜːvɪs ˈeɪdʒənt]	sb who solves customers' problems	Kundendienstmitarbeiter/in
	medical technician	[ˌmedɪkl tekˈnɪʃn]	sb who works in a lab and tests blood	Medizintechniker/in
	syringe	[sɪˈrɪndʒ]	sth that is used to take blood	Spritze
	stamp	[stæmp]	sth you get in your passport in some countries	Stempel
	saw	[sɔː]	sth a carpenter uses to cut wood	Säge
	spanner	[ˈspænə]	sth a mechanic uses to repair cars	Schraubenschlüssel
	uniform	[ˈjuːnɪfɔːm]	e.g. school uniform, police uniform, etc.	Dienstkleidung, Uniform
	canteen	[kænˈtiːn]	the place people go for lunch in companies	Kantine
36	to **show sb around**	[ˌʃəʊ əˈraʊnd]	e.g. He showed me around on my first day.	jdn herumführen
	Best of luck!	[ˌbest əv ˈlʌk]	e.g. Best of luck! Everything will be fine.	Alles Gute! Viel Glück!
	sales manager	[ˈseɪlz mænɪdʒə]	the boss of the sales department	Vertriebsleiter/in
	to **be in a rush**	[bi ɪn ə ˈrʌʃ]	to be in a hurry	in Eile sein, es eilig haben
	floor plan	[ˈflɔː plæn]	e.g. Look at the floor plan if you get lost.	Grundriss, Raumplan
	tasty	[ˈteɪsti]	*v* to taste	lecker
	product development	[ˌprɒdʌkt dɪˈveləpmənt]	e.g. New products come from product development.	Produktentwicklung
	recipe	[ˈresəpi]	e.g. Try this new recipe for cheese bread.	Rezept
	alive	[əˈlaɪv]	<> dead	lebendig
	packing	[ˈpækɪŋ]	*v* to pack	Verpackung
	shipping	[ˈʃɪpɪŋ]	*v* to ship	Versand
	lorry *BE*	[ˈlɒri]	e.g. There are lots of lorries on the motorway.	Lastwagen, Lkw
	marketing	[ˈmɑːkɪtɪŋ]	*v* to market sth	Vermarktung, Marketing
	accounts *pl*	[əˈkaʊnts]	department which looks after money	Buchhaltung
	view	[vjuː]	e.g. The view from the top was amazing.	Aussicht
	corridor	[ˈkɒrɪdɔː]	e.g. There are lots of corridors in this building.	Flur, Gang
	to **be all smiles**	[bi ˌɔːl ˈsmaɪlz]	to be very happy	über das ganze Gesicht strahlen
37	**ground floor** *BE*	[ˌgraʊnd ˈflɔː]	e.g. The entrance is on the ground floor.	Erdgeschoss
	first floor *AE*	[ˌfɜːst ˈflɔː]	e.g. Americans call the ground floor the first floor.	Erdgeschoss
	to **sign sth**	[saɪn]	to write your name on sth	etw unterzeichnen
	to **pick sb/sth up**	[ˌpɪk ˈʌp]	to collect sb/sth	jdn/etw abholen
	door entry card	[ˈdɔːr entri kɑːd]	e.g. Hotels use door entry cards instead of keys.	Zugangskarte
	straight ahead	[ˌstreɪt əˈhed]	e.g. Go straight ahead, don't turn left or right.	geradeaus
38	**trial period**	[ˌtraɪəl ˈpɪəriəd]	e.g. The trial period is the first few months of a job.	Probezeit
	Have a seat.	[həv ə ˈsiːt]	Please sit down.	Nehmen Sie Platz!
	to **be short of sth**	[bi ˈʃɔːt əv]	to not have enough of sth	zu wenig(e) von etw haben
	… I'm afraid …	[aɪm əˈfreɪd]	e.g. I'm afraid we haven't got any more tickets.	leider, ich fürchte
39	**careers advice**	[kəˌrɪəz ədˈvaɪs]	e.g. We were given good careers advice.	Berufsberatung
	to **quit**	[kwɪt]	to leave your job	kündigen
40	**jobseeker**	[ˈdʒɒbsiːkə]	sb who is looking for a job	Arbeitssuchende/r
	home care	[ˌhəʊm ˈkeə]	e.g. Old or sick people often have home care.	häusliche Krankenpflege
	shift	[ʃɪft]	e.g. Nurses work shifts, sometimes during the day, sometimes at night.	Schicht
	to **deliver a baby**	[dɪˌlɪvər ə ˈbeɪbi]	e.g. Doctors deliver babies in hospitals.	ein Kind zur Welt bringen

	drive	[draɪv]	*v* to drive	Autofahrt
	to **give sb a check-up**	[ˌgɪv ə ˈtʃekʌp]	to check if sb is OK	jdn untersuchen
	meditating	[ˈmedɪteɪtɪŋ]	e.g. Meditating helps me think.	Meditieren
	to **log into sth**	[ˈlɒg ɪntə]	to sign into a computer programme or app	sich in etw einloggen
	to **take a call**	[ˌteɪk ə ˈkɔːl]	to answer the phone	einen Anruf entgegennehmen
	insurance	[ɪnˈʃʊərəns]	*v* to insure	Versicherung
	to **do the laundry**	[duː ðə ˈlɔːndri]	to do the washing	Wäsche waschen
	follow-up	[ˈfɒləʊ ʌp]	e.g. It's good to make a follow-up call to a customer.	Nachbereitung, Nachfassen
	marine electrician	[məˌriːn ɪlekˈtrɪʃn]	sb who works on the electrics in a boat or ship	Schiffselektriker/in
	electrics	[ɪˈlektrɪks]	e.g. The electrics in a boat are very complicated.	Elektrik
	electronics	[ˌɪlekˈtrɒnɪks]	e.g. You have to know a lot to understand electronics.	Elektronik
	solar panel	[ˌsəʊlə ˈpænl]	e.g. We have got solar panels on our roof to generate electricity.	Solarmodul
	boatyard	[ˈbəʊtjɑːd]	a place where boats are repaired	Bootswerft
	spare part	[ˌspeə ˈpɑːt]	sth you need when sth breaks	Ersatzteil
	warehouse	[ˈweəhaʊs]	a big building where they keep lots of things	Lager
	watermaker	[ˈwɔːtəmeɪkə]	a machine for making clean water	Wasseraufbereitungsanlage, Entsalzer
41	**battery**	[ˈbætəri]	e.g. Mobile phones need batteries.	Akku, Batterie
	to **dress informally**	[ˌdres ɪnˈfɔːməli]	to dress casually	sich leger kleiden
	to **skip sth**	[skɪp]	to miss sth	etw auslassen, auf etw verzichten
	acceptable	[əkˈseptəbl]	*v* to accept	akzeptabel
	guideline	[ˈgaɪdlaɪn]	e.g. Read the guidelines before you start.	Vorgabe, Richtlinie, Hinweis
	appropriate	[əˈprəʊpriət]	e.g. I think this is an appropriate salary.	angemessen, geeignet
	to **belong somewhere**	[bɪˈlɒŋ]	e.g. This book belongs on the shelf.	wohin gehören
	stain	[steɪn]	*v* to stain	Schmutzfleck
	risky	[ˈrɪski]	*n* risk	riskant, gefährlich
	plain	[pleɪn]	e.g. Plain colours are better for the office.	einfarbig, schlicht
	tight	[taɪt]	e.g. Don't wear tight skirts or trousers in the office.	*(Kleidung:)* enganliegend, knapp
42	**(production) plant**	[plɑːnt]	e.g. A new plant opened on the other side of town.	Werk, Fabrik
	as a result	[əz ə rɪˈzʌlt]	e.g. It's all as a result of pollution.	folglich, infolgedessen
	pharmaceutical company	[fɑːməˌsuːtɪkl ˈkʌmpəni]	a company that makes medicines	Pharmaunternehmen
	sales *pl*	[seɪlz]	the money a company makes from selling products	Umsatz
	for now	[fə ˈnaʊ]	e.g. Let's leave it there for now and do it later.	einstweilen, erst einmal
43	**open day**	[ˈəʊpən deɪ]	e.g. There is a school open day on Saturday.	Tag der offenen Tür
	extract	[ˈekstrækt]	e.g. Read this extract from the novel.	Auszug, Ausschnitt
	(bank) balance	[ˈbæləns]	e.g. Your bank balance tells you how much money you have.	Kontostand, Saldo
	to **work out OK**	[wɜːk ˌaʊt əʊ ˈkeɪ]	to be OK in the end	sich von alleine regeln/ erledigen
	to **interview for sth**	[ˈɪntəvjuː fə]	*n* interview	Vorstellungsgespräche für etw führen
	outline	[ˈaʊtlaɪn]	e.g. Write an outline of your story first.	Gliederung, Entwurf
	fascinated	[ˈfæsɪneɪtɪd]	*n* fascination	fasziniert
	Too bad!	[ˌtuː ˈbæd]	You were unlucky!	Pech gehabt!
	unprepared	[ʌnprɪˈpeəd]	<> prepared	unvorbereitet
	disorganized	[dɪsˈɔːgənaɪzd]	<> organized	unorganisiert, schlecht organisiert
	summer job	[ˈsʌmə dʒɒb]	e.g. A summer job is good to earn some money.	Ferienjob
44	**chocolate maker**	[ˈtʃɒklət meɪkə]	sb who makes things with chocolate	Chocolatier/-ière

UNIT 5

45	**alternative**	[ɔːlˈtɜːnətɪv]	different option	Alternative
	flour	[ˈflaʊə]	sth you use to bake a cake	Mehl
	soap	[səʊp]	sth you use to wash yourself with	Seife
	coconut	[ˈkəʊkənʌt]	a tropical fruit	Kokosnuss
	lid	[lɪd]	the top that closes a jar or bottle	Deckel

	stick	[stɪk]	e.g. Do you need a stick to stir your coffee?	Stab
	to **stir sth**	[stɜː]	to mix sth	etw umrühren
46	to **ban sth**	[bæn]	to not allow sth	etw verbieten
	single-use	[ˌsɪŋgl ˈjuːs]	<> multi-use	Einweg-
	sb cares about sth	[ˈkeəz əbaʊt]	sb thinks sth is important	jdm liegt etw am Herzen
	final decision	[ˌfaɪnl dɪˈsɪʒn]	*v* to decide	endgültige Entscheidung
	to **go ahead with sth**	[ˌgəʊ əˈhed wɪð]	to start (sth)	etw durchführen, etw machen
	If I were you …	[ɪf ˌaɪ wə ˈjuː]	e.g. If I were you, I would take the job.	an deiner/Ihrer Stelle
	water cooler	[ˈwɔːtə kuːlə]	where you can get cold water to drink	Trinkwasserspender
	tap water	[ˈtæp wɔːtə]	<> bottled water	Leitungswasser
	straw	[strɔː]	e.g. Do you want a straw for your lemonade?	Strohhalm
	takeaway	[ˈteɪkəweɪ]	e.g. I ordered the pizza to takeaway.	*(Essen:)* zum Mitnehmen
	wooden	[ˈwʊdn]	made from wood	aus Holz
	reusable	[ˌriːˈjuːzəbl]	<> disposable	wiederverwendbar
	capsule	[ˈkæpsjuːl]	e.g. a coffee capsule	Kapsel
	talk	[tɔːk]	e.g. There were some interesting talks at the training course.	Vortrag
	pollution	[pəˈluːʃn]	*v* to pollute	Verschmutzung
	habit	[ˈhæbɪt]	sth you do regularly	Gewohnheit
	waste collection	[ˈweɪst kəˈlekʃn]	*v* to collect waste	Müllabfuhr
	to **calculate sth**	[ˈkælkjuleɪt]	*n* calculation	etw berechnen, etw ausrechnen
	amount	[əˈmaʊnt]	quantity	Menge
	reputation	[ˌrepjuˈteɪʃn]	e.g. She has a reputation for being late. She's never on time!	Ruf
	ban	[bæn]	when you are not allowed to do sth	Verbot
47	**billion**	[ˈbɪliən]	1,000,000,000	Milliarde
	trillion	[ˈtrɪljən]	1,000,000,000,000	Billion
	3D printing	[ˌθriː diː ˈprɪntɪŋ]	when you make sth using a 3D printer	3D-Druck
	to **sort sth into sth**	[ˈsɔːt ɪntə]	to group sth	etw nach etw sortieren
	bamboo	[ˌbæmˈbuː]	a type of wood	Bambus
48	**spare time**	[ˌspeə ˈtaɪm]	leisure time, free time	Freizeit
	module	[ˈmɒdjuːl]	a part of a training course	Modul
	to **market sth**	[ˈmɑːkɪt]	to advertise sth to a particular group	etw vermarkten
	to **be suspicious of sth**	[bi səˈspɪʃəs əv]	to distrust sth	einer Sache gegenüber misstrauisch sein
	technique	[tekˈniːk]	way of doing sth	Methode, Technik
	genuinely	[ˈdʒenjuɪnli]	actually, really	wirklich, ernsthaft
	to **advertise sth**	[ˈædvətaɪz]	*n* advertisement	für etw Werbung machen, etw bewerben
	as a whole	[əz ə ˈhəʊl]	e.g. Think about the business as a whole, not just your department.	als Ganzes
	organic	[ɔːˈgænɪk]	e.g. organic food, organic farming	Bio-
	to **highlight sth**	[ˈhaɪlaɪt]	to make sth stand out, to emphasize sth	etw hervorheben
	to **apply for sth**	[əˈplaɪ fə]	e.g. to apply for a club membership	etw beantragen
	environmental label	[ɪnvaɪrənˌmentl ˈleɪbl]	sth that shows that your product is environmentally friendly	Umweltsiegel
	industry	[ˈɪndəstri]	e.g. the car industry, the tourist industry, etc.	Branche
	to **invest**	[ɪnˈvest]	to put money into sth	investieren
	to **carry sth out**	[ˌkæri ˈaʊt]	to do sth	etw durchführen, etw in die Tat umsetzen
	to **connect to sth**	[kəˈnekt tə]	*n* connection	eine emotionale Verbindung zu etw herstellen
49	**marketer**	[ˈmɑːkɪtə]	sb who organizes marketing	Vermarkter/in, Marketingfachmann/-frau
	campaign	[kæmˈpeɪn]	e.g. a marketing or advertising campaign	Kampagne, Aktion
	consumer	[kənˈsjuːmə]	*v* to consume	Verbraucher/in
	obviously	[ˈɒbviəsli]	clearly	natürlich
	to **convince sb of sth**	[kənˈvɪns əv]	to make sb believe sth	jdn von etw überzeugen
	to **promise**	[ˈprɒmɪs]	to say you will do sth	versprechen
	advertisement, advert, ad	[ədˈvɜːtɪsmənt, ˈædvɜːt, æd]	e.g. a job advert, an advert for clothing, etc.	Anzeige, Werbespot, Werbung
50	**greenhouse gases** *pl*	[ˌgriːnhaʊs ˈgæsɪz]	e.g. carbon dioxide and methane	Treibhausgase

	climate change	[ˈklaɪmət tʃeɪndʒ]	e.g. Be more environmentally friendly and stop climate change!	Klimawandel
	to **brush one's teeth**	[ˌbrʌʃ wʌnz ˈtiːθ]	to clean one's teeth	sich die Zähne putzen
	appliance	[əˈplaɪəns]	e.g. washing machine, dishwasher, microwave, etc.	Haushaltsgerät, Elektrogerät
	worth	[wɜːθ]	e.g. It may seem like hard work but it will be worth it in the end.	wert
	in the long run	[ɪn ðə lɒŋ ˈrʌn]	long-term <> short-term	langfristig, auf lange Sicht
	landfill	[ˈlændfɪl]	e.g. Throwaway plastic cups end up in landfill.	Mülldeponie
	leftover food	[ˌleftəʊvə ˈfuːd]	food that isn't eaten	Essensreste
	sell-by date	[sel baɪ ˈdeɪt]	e.g. The supermarket can't sell food that is past its sell-by date.	Haltbarkeitsdatum
	packet	[ˈpækɪt]	e.g. a packet of crisps or biscuits	Packung
	loose	[luːs]	not in a package or container	lose, unverpackt
	container	[kənˈteɪnə]	sth you put things in	Gefäß, Behälter
	to **be in season**	[bi ˌɪn ˈsiːzn]	e.g. Strawberries are only in season in the summer.	Saison haben
	light bulb	[ˈlaɪt bʌlb]	e.g. It's dark. Can you change the light bulb, please?	Glühbirne
	recyclable	[ˌriːˈsaɪkləbl]	<> non-recyclable	wiederverwertbar, recyclebar
	jam jar	[ˈdʒæm dʒɑː]	e.g. Reuse your old jam jars, don't throw them away.	Marmeladenglas
51	**century**	[ˈsentʃəri]	a hundred years	Jahrhundert
	to **walk past sth**	[ˌwɔːk ˈpɑːst]	e.g. We walk past the shop on the way to school every day.	an etw vorbeilaufen
	tap	[tæp]	e.g. tap water	Wasserhahn
	cloth	[klɒθ]	e.g. We use cloth bags for our shopping, not plastic bags.	Stoff, Tuch
	to **pick sth up**	[ˌpɪk ˈʌp]	<> to drop sth	etw aufheben
	rubbish bin	[ˈrʌbɪʃ bɪn]	where you put things you want to throw away	Abfalleimer, Mülltonne
	automatically	[ˌɔːtəˈmætɪkli]	<> manually	automatisch
	to **switch sth on**	[ˌswɪtʃ ˈɒn]	to turn sth on <> to turn/switch sth off	etw einschalten
	LED bulb	[ˌel iː ˈdiː bʌlb]	e.g. LED bulbs are better for the environment than other light bulbs.	LED-Leuchte, LED
	voice message	[ˈvɔɪs mesɪdʒ]	e.g. I don't like writing text messages so I send voice messages instead.	Sprachnachricht
52	**line graph**	[ˈlaɪn grɑːf]	e.g. The line graph shows how sales have increased.	Liniendiagramm, Kurvendiagramm
	sales figures *pl*	[ˈseɪlz fɪgəz]	numbers showing how many things you have sold	Verkaufszahlen, Umsatzzahlen
	to **climb**	[klaɪm]	to go up	steigen, nach oben klettern
	to **decrease**	[dɪˈkriːs]	to go down <> to increase	abnehmen, sinken
	to **drop**	[drɒp]	to go down	fallen
	to **increase**	[ɪnˈkriːs]	to go up <> to decrease	steigen, zunehmen
	to **rise**	[raɪz]	to go up	ansteigen
	quarter	[ˈkwɔːtə]	period of three months	Quartal
	dramatical(ly)	[drəˈmætɪkl]	radical(ly)	dramatisch
	previous	[ˈpriːviəs]	before, earlier	vorig, vorhergehend
	impact	[ˈɪmpækt]	effect, consequence	Auswirkung(en), Folge(n)
53	**total**	[ˈtəʊtl]	e.g. The total price of your order is ten pounds.	Gesamt-
	cosmetics *pl*	[kɒzˈmetɪks]	make-up	Kosmetik(artikel)
	to **deal with sth**	[ˈdiːl wɪð]	e.g. This graph deals with how sales have grown over the last year.	sich mit etw beschäftigen, etw zum Gegenstand haben
	axis	[ˈæksɪs]	e.g. x or y axis on a graph	Achse
	competition	[ˌkɒmpəˈtɪʃn]	*v* to compete	(die) Konkurrenz
54	**happiness**	[ˈhæpinəs]	<> sadness	Glück, Zufriedenheit
	diet	[ˈdaɪət]	what you eat	Ernährung, Kost
	to **support sth**	[səˈpɔːt]	<> to be against sth	etw *(Argument usw.)* untermauern, etw stärken
	shopper	[ˈʃɒpə]	customer	Kunde/Kundin *(im Einzelhandel)*
	I see your point.	[aɪˌ siː jɔː ˈpɔɪnt]	I understand what you mean.	Ich verstehe, worauf Sie hinauswollen.
	contribution	[ˌkɒntrɪˈbjuːʃn]	*v* to contribute	Beitrag

UNIT 6

55	to **push in**	[ˌpʊʃ ˈɪn]	e.g. Don't push in. We're all waiting in this line.	sich vordrängeln
	damaged	[ˈdæmɪdʒd]	broken, faulty	beschädigt
	to **break**	[breɪk]	<> to fix	kaputtgehen
	to **deliver sth**	[dɪˈlɪvə]	*n* delivery	etw liefern, etw zustellen
56	**immigrant**	[ˈɪmɪgrənt]	sb who has moved to a new country	Einwanderer/-in
	special class	[ˌspeʃl ˈklɑːs]	e.g. We have special classes to teach new immigrants English.	Förderkurs
	retired	[rɪˈtaɪəd]	*v* to retire	im Ruhestand, pensioniert
	to **review sth**	[rɪˈvjuː]	to reconsider sth	etw erneut prüfen, etw überprüfen
57	**brochure**	[ˈbrəʊʃə]	e.g. Our brochure tells you all about the school and what makes it special.	Prospekt
	to **take place**	[ˌteɪk ˈpleɪs]	e.g. Halloween takes place on 31st October every year.	stattfinden
	to **state**	[steɪt]	to say, to explain	sagen, angeben, behaupten
58	**complaint**	[kəmˈpleɪnt]	*v* to complain	Beschwerde, Reklamation, Klage
	to **catch sth**	[kætʃ]	e.g. to catch a cold, to catch a bus, ...	etw kriegen, etw erwischen
59	**apology**	[əˈpɒlədʒi]	*v* to apologise	Entschuldigung
	dead	[ded]	<> alive	tot
	to **stand up**	[ˌstænd ˈʌp]	<> to sit down	aufstehen
	bench	[bentʃ]	a place outside to sit down	Bank
60	**cultural**	[ˈkʌltʃərəl]	*n* culture	kulturell
	misunderstanding	[ˌmɪsʌndəˈstændɪŋ]	confusion, problem	Missverständnis
	dish	[dɪʃ]	e.g. We eat lots of small dishes for dinner instead of one big meal.	*(Essen:)* Gericht
	bowl	[bəʊl]	e.g. Put the soup in the bowls over there.	Schale, Schüssel
	alcoholic	[ˌælkəˈhɒlɪk]	sb who drinks too much alcohol	Alkoholiker/in
	lucky number	[ˌlʌki ˈnʌmbə]	e.g. Two is a lucky number in China.	Glückszahl
	sb has a hard time doing sth	[həz ə ˌhɑːd ˈtaɪm]	sth is difficult for sb	jdm fällt es schwer, etw zu tun
	punctual	[ˈpʌŋktʃuəl]	<> late	pünktlich
	to **adapt (to sth)**	[əˈdæpt]	to change to fit in with sth	sich (an etw) anpassen, sich an etw gewöhnen
	to **separate sth**	[ˈsepəreɪt]	to keep sth apart	etw trennen
61	to **nod the head**	[ˌnɒd ðə ˈhed]	<> to shake the head	mit dem Kopf nicken
	to **refuse sth**	[rɪˈfjuːz]	to say no to sth	etw ablehnen
	insulting	[ɪnˈsʌltɪŋ]	*v* to insult sb	beleidigend
	plate	[pleɪt]	e.g. The sandwich can go on that plate.	Teller
	thumb	[θʌm]	e.g. You have eight fingers and two thumbs.	Daumen
	strict	[strɪkt]	<> relaxed	streng
	to **offend sb**	[əˈfend]	*adj* offensive	jdn kränken, jdn beleidigen
	disrespectful	[ˌdɪsrɪˈspektfl]	*n* respect	respektlos
	tip	[tɪp]	money you give a waiter for example after a meal	Trinkgeld
	service	[ˈsɜːvɪs]	e.g. If the service is good, you should give the waiter a good tip.	Dienstleistung
62	**bold**	[bəʊld]	e.g. The words in bold are often important.	fettgedruckt
	hairdryer	[ˈheədraɪə]	machine you use to dry your hair	Föhn
	to **hang on a minute**	[ˌhæŋ ˈɒn ə mɪnɪt]	to wait a minute	kurz warten
	to **dry**	[draɪ]	<> to get wet	trocknen
	to **be designed for sb/sth**	[bi dɪˈzaɪnd fə]	e.g. The website is designed for people who can't read very well.	für jdn/etw gedacht sein, sich an jdn/etw richten
	depending on sth	[dɪˈpendɪŋ ɒn]	e.g. There are lots of options depending on how much you want to pay.	je nachdem ..., abhängig von etw
63	to **mediate**	[ˈmiːdieɪt]	e.g. She can't speak English so I mediated for her.	vermitteln
	to **overreact**	[ˌəʊvərɪˈækt]	e.g. I think I overreacted. The problem wasn't really that bad.	überreagieren
64	to **rate sth**	[reɪt]	to say how good sth is	etw bewerten
	to **cover sth**	[ˈkʌvə]	e.g. The report coveres all the important points.	etw *(Thema usw.)* behandeln
	rating	[ˈreɪtɪŋ]	e.g. This film has a good rating. Let's watch it!	Bewertung

UNIT 7

65	**yet**	[jet]	e.g. We haven't decided what to do yet.	schon
	service	[ˈsɜːvɪs]	*v* to service sth	Wartung, Inspektion
	diary	[ˈdaɪəri]	e.g. I write all my appointments in my diary.	Kalender
	brake	[breɪk]	*v* to brake	Bremse
66	to **make arrangements**	[meɪk əˈreɪndʒmənts]	to arrange sth	Vorbereitungen treffen, Termine ausmachen, Buchungen vornehmen
	trade fair	[ˈtreɪd feə]	e.g. You can speak to trade customers at trade fairs.	Messe, Fachmesse, Branchenmesse
	to **fly in**	[ˌflaɪ ˈɪn]	to arrive by plane	*(mit dem Flugzeug)* ankommen
	to **message sb**	[ˈmesɪdʒ]	to send sb a message	jdm eine Nachricht schicken, sich bei jdm melden
	spicy	[ˈspaɪsi]	sth made with lots of spices	pikant, würzig, scharf
	plenty of	[ˈplenti əv]	lots of, many, much, …	viel, genügend
67	to **pay sb/sth a visit**	[peɪ ə ˈvɪzɪt]	to visit sb/sth	jdm/etw einen Besuch abstatten
68	**return journey**	[rɪˈtɜːn dʒɜːni]	<> single journey	Rückfahrt
	to **work out**	[ˌwɜːk ˈaʊt]	to go, to happen	laufen, sich ergeben
	housekeeper	[ˈhaʊskiːpə]	sb in a hotel in charge of the rooms	*(Hotel:)* Reinigungskraft
	to **stay with sb**	[ˈsteɪ wɪð]	to visit sb and stay over night	bei jdm übernachten
	to **check out**	[ˌtʃek ˈaʊt]	*n* check out	abreisen, auschecken
	charge	[tʃɑːdʒ]	fee, *v* to charge	Gebühr
	to **go off duty**	[gəʊ ˌɒf ˈdjuːti]	to finish your shift	Dienstschluss haben
69	**line**	[laɪn]	e.g. Please hold the line and I'll check.	Leitung, Verbindung
	seat	[siːt]	*v* to sit (down)	Platz, Sitz
	to **check in one's bags**	[tʃek ˌɪn wʌnz ˈbægz]	e.g. You have to check in your bags two hours before the plane leaves.	sein Gepäck aufgeben
	boarding pass	[ˈbɔːdɪŋ pɑːs]	e.g. You need a boarding pass to get on a plane.	Bordkarte
	delay	[dɪˈleɪ]	*v* to be delayed	Verspätung, Verzögerung
	gate	[geɪt]	e.g. Our plane leaves from gate A12.	Flugsteig, Gate
	immigration	[ˌɪmɪˈgreɪʃn]	*v* to immigrate	Passkontrolle
	security	[sɪˈkjʊərəti]	where your bags are checked before you fly	*(Flughafen usw.:)* Sicherheitskontrolle
	rebooking fee	[riːˈbʊkɪŋ fiː]	e.g. I have to pay a rebooking fee to change my flight.	Umbuchungsgebühr
70	**territory**	[ˈterətri]	e.g. Canada has provinces and territories.	Gebiet
	whale hunter	[ˈweɪl hʌntə]	sb who hunts whales	Walfänger/in
	to **canoe**	[kəˈnuː]	*n* canoe	mit dem Kanu fahren
	dog team	[ˈdɒg tiːm]	a group of dogs that pull a sled	Hundegespann
	to **go sledding**	[ˌgəʊ ˈsledɪŋ]	to sled	mit dem Hundeschlitten fahren
	province	[ˈprɒvɪns]	e.g. Provinces are like states.	Provinz
	competition	[ˌkɒmpəˈtɪʃn]	*v* to compete	Wettbewerb
	to **immigrate**	[ˈɪmɪgreɪt]	*n* immigrant	einwandern
	prairie	[ˈpreəri]	huge areas of flat land with grass and trees	Steppe, Prärie
	on one's doorstep	[ˌɒn wʌnz ˈdɔːstep]	very close to where you live	vor der (eigenen) Tür
	glacier	[ˈglæsiə]	a river that is frozen and moves very slowly	Gletscher
71	**capital**	[ˈkæpɪtl]	e.g. The capital of England is London.	Hauptstadt
	within	[wɪˈðɪn]	e.g. I found a job within a month.	innerhalb von
	immigration	[ˌɪmɪˈgreɪʃn]	*v* to immigrate	Einwanderung
	competitor	[kəmˈpetɪtə]	*v* to compete	Konkurrent/in
	new arrival	[ˌnjuː əˈraɪvl]	<> sb who has lived somewhere all their life	Neuankömmling
	liveable	[ˈlɪvəbl]	*v* to live	lebenswert
	frozen lake	[ˌfrəʊzn ˈleɪk]	e.g. There are many frozen lakes in Canada in the winter.	zugefrorener See
	maple syrup	[ˌmeɪpl ˈsɪrəp]	e.g. Canadians like maple syrup on their pancakes.	Ahornsirup
	national flag	[ˌnæʃnl ˈflæg]	e.g. The Canadian national flag is red and has a maple leaf on it.	Nationalflagge
	to **apologize to sb**	[əˈpɒlədʒaɪz tə]	*n* apology	sich bei jdm entschuldigen
72	**minutes** *pl*	[ˈmɪnɪts]	e.g. It's my turn to write the minutes of the meeting.	Protokoll
	invention	[ɪnˈvenʃn]	*v* to invent	Erfindung
	innovation	[ˌɪnəˈveɪʃn]	*v* to innovate	Neuerung, Innovation
	specifications *pl*	[ˌspesɪfɪˈkeɪʃnz]	*v* to specify	technische Daten

73	to **be off sick**	[bi ˌɒf ˈsɪk]	to miss work because you are ill	krankgeschrieben sein
	to **be amazed at sth**	[bi əˈmeɪzd ət]	*adj* amazing	über etw erstaunt sein
	fact-finding	[ˈfækt faɪndɪŋ]	e.g. It was a real fact-finding trip to the factory.	Erkundung
	to **collect sth**	[kəˈlekt]	*n* collection	etw sammeln
	to **refer back to sth**	[rɪˌfɜː ˈbæk tə]	e.g. I refer back to my notes when I write the minutes.	auf etw zurückkommen
74	to **entertain sb**	[ˌentəˈteɪn]	*n* entertainment	jdn bewirten, jdn unterhalten
	to **depart**	[dɪˈpɑːt]	*n* departure	abreisen

UNIT 8

75	to **finance sth**	[ˈfaɪnæns]	*adj* financial	etw finanzieren
	to **hire sb**	[ˈhaɪə]	to give sb a job	jdn engagieren
76	**financial planning**	[faɪˌnænʃl ˈplænɪŋ]	to plan what you can spend your money on	Finanzplanung
	to **budget sth**	[ˈbʌdʒɪt]	*n* budget	sich etw *(Geld usw.)* einteilen, mit etw sparsam umgehen
	savings account	[ˈseɪvɪŋz əkaʊnt]	e.g. I put money in my savings account so I can buy a car next year.	Sparkonto
	emergency fund	[ɪˈmɜːdʒənsi fʌnd]	e.g. An emergency fund is a good idea if you have a car.	Notfallfonds, Rücklagen für Notfälle
	to **be tired of sth**	[bi ˈtaɪəd əv]	to be fed up of sth	etw leid sein, etw satthaben
	shiny	[ˈʃaɪni]	clean and without any damage	glänzend, blitzblank
	to **borrow sth**	[ˈbɒrəʊ]	<> to lend sth	sich etw leihen
	to **pay cash**	[ˌpeɪ ˈkæʃ]	<> to pay with a credit card	bar zahlen
	petrol	[ˈpetrəl]	e.g. We need to put some petrol in the car today.	Benzin
	used car	[juːzd ˈkɑː]	<> new car	Gebrauchtwagen
	long-term	[ˌlɒŋˈtɜːm]	<> short-term	langfristig
	to **look closely at sth**	[ˌlʊk ˈkləʊsli ət]	to read sth very carefully	sich etw genau ansehen
77	**loan**	[ləʊn]	money you borrow from sb or a bank	Kredit
78	to **deal with sth**	[ˈdiːl wɪð]	to handle sth	mit etw umgehen
	banking	[ˈbæŋkɪŋ]	*v* to bank	Bankgeschäfte
	to **celebrate in style**	[ˌselɪbreɪt ɪn ˈstaɪl]	*n* (a big) celebration	groß feiern
	currency exchange	[ˌkʌrənsi ɪksˈtʃeɪndʒ]	e.g. We changed our euros into pounds at the currency exchange office.	Geldumtausch, Währungsumtausch
	exchange rate	[ɪksˈtʃeɪndʒ reɪt]	e.g. There is a good exchange rate for euros today.	Wechselkurs
	change	[tʃeɪndʒ]	*v* to change	Wechselgeld
	to **burn sth**	[bɜːn]	e.g. I burnt my finger while cooking.	etw verbrennen
	application form	[ˌæplɪˈkeɪʃn fɔːm]	e.g. Fill in the application form first, please.	Antragsformular
	bank transfer	[ˈbæŋk trænsfɜː]	when you send money from one bank to another	Überweisung
	digit	[ˈdɪdʒɪt]	digits on a credit card are the numbers on it	Ziffer
	expiry date	[ɪkˈspaɪəri deɪt]	the date that a credit card can't be used after	Ablaufdatum
79	**budgeting**	[ˈbʌdʒɪtɪŋ]	*v* to budget sth	Haushaltsplanung, Finanzplanung
	budget	[ˈbʌdʒɪt]	e.g. My monthly budget isn't very much.	Haushalt, Budget, Etat
	expenses *pl*	[ɪkˈspensɪz]	the money you spend on things	Ausgaben
	category	[ˈkætəgəri]	e.g. group, topic, theme	Rubrik, Kategorie, Gruppe
	wants *pl*	[wɒnts]	*v* to want	Wünsche
	savings *pl*	[ˈseɪvɪŋz]	*v* to save	Ersparnisse
	debts *pl*	[dets]	e.g. I don't want to have any debts yet.	Schulden
	rent	[rent]	*v* to rent	Miete
	eating out	[ˌiːtɪŋ ˈaʊt]	e.g. I love eating out with my partner.	essen gehen
	to **try hard**	[ˌtraɪ ˈhɑːd]	to do everything you can to make sth work	sich (große) Mühe geben
80	**fully furnished**	[ˌfʊli ˈfɜːnɪʃt]	when all the furniture is already in a room/flat	komplett möbliert
	utilities *pl*	[juːˈtɪlətiz]	e.g. gas, electricity, telephone costs	Nebenkosten
	shared	[ʃeəd]	e.g. We all pay for the utilities, they are shared costs.	gemeinsam (genutzt)
	to **cover sth**	[ˈkʌvə]	*n* cover	etw *(Kosten usw.)* decken
	to **share (a flat) with sb**	[ˈʃeə wɪð]	e.g. I share a flat with my best friend.	mit jdm zusammenwohnen
	to **get used to sth**	[get ˈjuːs(t) tə]	e.g. We got used to the noise from the street.	sich an etw gewöhnen
	regular	[ˈregjələ]	<> irregular	normal

81	**review**	[rɪ'vjuː]	*v* to review	Kritik, Rezension, Besprechung
	manager	['mænɪdʒə]	sb who manages things for others	Verwalter/in
	sb **realized** sth	['rɪəlaɪzɪz]	e.g. He realized his mistake too late.	jdm wird etw klar
	management	['mænɪdʒmənt]	*v* to manage sth	Verwaltung
	sense of family	[ˌsens əv 'fæmli]	when everyone feels close as if they are related	familiäres Miteinander
	virtual	['vɜːtʃuəl]	<> real, actual	virtuell
	to **hit one's head on sth**	[ˌhɪt wʌnz 'hed ɒn]	e.g. The room was small and I hit my head on things.	sich den Kopf an etw stoßen
	landlord	['lændlɔːd]	sb who owns the flat/house you live in	Vermieter
	deposit	[dɪ'pɒzɪt]	e.g. We had to pay three months' rent as a deposit.	Kaution
	roommate	['ruːmmeɪt]	the person you live with	Mitbewohner/in
	agreement	[ə'griːmənt]	*v* to agree	Vereinbarung
	in writing	[ɪn 'raɪtɪŋ]	e.g. We were given our grades in writing.	schriftlich
	balcony	['bælkəni]	e.g. The balcony in the flat was tiny.	Balkon
	parking space	['pɑːkɪŋ speɪs]	where you can park your car	Parkplatz
	lift	[lɪft]	e.g. The flat is on the fourth floor and there isn't a lift.	Aufzug, Fahrstuhl
	unfurnished	[ʌn'fɜːnɪʃt]	<> furnished	unmöbliert
83	**i.e. (= that is)**	[ˌaɪ 'iː]	e.g. We had more work, i.e. more meetings.	d.h. (= das heißt, nämlich)
	overtime	['əʊvətaɪm]	hours you work more than you are supposed to	Überstunden
	grid	[grɪd]	e.g. table, chart	Raster
	to **tick** sth	[tɪk]	e.g. If you agree, tick the box.	etw abhaken, etw mit einem Häkchen versehen
	net	[net]	e.g. My net salary isn't very much.	netto
	to **estimate sth**	['estɪmeɪt]	to guess sth	etw schätzen
	to **share sth with sb**	['ʃeə wɪð]	e.g. We shared the chocolates that were left.	sich etw mit jdm teilen
	heating	['hiːtɪŋ]	*v* to heat	Heizung

Video Wortliste

Video 1

industry	['ɪndəstri]	Branche
summer job	['sʌmə dʒɒb]	Ferienjob
reference	['refərəns]	Referenz
to **apply for sth**	[ə'plaɪ fə]	sich für/um etw bewerben

Video 2

to **look hard at sb/sth**	[ˌlʊk 'hɑːd ət]	jdn/etw genau unter die Lupe nehmen
to **look closely at sth**	[ˌlʊk 'kləʊsli ət]	sich etw genau ansehen
to **be an introvert**	[bi ən 'ɪntrəvɜːt]	introvertiert sein
to **be an extrovert**	[bi ən 'ekstrəvɜːt]	extrovertiert sein

Video 3

face-to-face	[ˌfeɪs tə 'feɪs]	persönlich
printout	['prɪntaʊt]	Ausdruck
straight back	[ˌstreɪt 'bæk]	gerader Rücken
volume	['vɒljuːm]	Lautstärke
delay	[dɪ'leɪ]	Verzögerung
to **pause**	[pɔːz]	warten, pausieren

Video 4

timetable	['taɪmteɪbl]	Fahrplan
route	[ruːt]	Strecke
at once	[ət 'wʌns]	sofort
to **keep sb waiting**	[kiːp 'weɪtɪŋ]	jdn warten lassen

Video 5

habit	['hæbɪt]	Gewohnheit
to **inspire sb to do sth**	[ɪn'spaɪə]	jdn dazu anregen, etw zu tun
to **collect sth**	[kə'lekt]	etw sammeln
to **cut sth**	[kʌt]	etw vermeiden, etw senken
bottled	['bɒtld]	in Flaschen
washable	['wɒʃəbl]	waschbar
container	[kən'teɪnə]	Gefäß, Behälter
to **advertise sth**	['ædvətaɪz]	für etw Werbung machen, etw bewerben

Video 6

service	['sɜːvɪs]	Dienstleistung
smell	[smel]	Geruch, Gestank
to **handle sb/sth**	['hændl]	mit jdm/etw umgehen
What's the point of ...?	[ˌwɒts ðə 'pɔɪnt əv]	Welchen Sinn hat ...?
to **fix sth**	[fɪks]	etw reparieren
to **follow up**	[ˌfɒləʊ 'ʌp]	nachfassen

Video 7

border	['bɔːdə]	Grenze
population	[ˌpɒpju'leɪʃn]	Bevölkerung
glacier	['glæsiə]	Gletscher
diamond	['daɪəmənd]	Diamant
producer	[prə'djuːsə]	Produzent/in
wilderness	['wɪldənəs]	Wildnis
to **camp**	[kæmp]	zelten
to **fish**	[fɪʃ]	angeln
to **canoe**	[kə'nuː]	mit dem Kanu fahren
Arctic Circle	[ˌɑːktɪk 'sɜːkl]	Polarkreis
to **get caught in sth**	[ˌget 'kɔːt ɪn]	in etw stecken bleiben

Northern Lights *pl*	[ˌnɔːðən ˈlaɪts]	Polarlicht, Nordlicht
dog sled	[ˈdɒg sled]	Hundeschlitten
spectacular	[spekˈtækjələ]	atemberaubend, spektakulär

Video 8

to **charge a fee**	[ˌtʃɑːdʒ ə ˈfiː]	eine Gebühr verlangen
interest	[ˈɪntrəst]	Zins(en)
branch	[brɑːntʃ]	Filiale, Zweigstelle
proof of address	[ˌpruːf əv əˈdres]	Adressnachweis
ID	[ˌaɪ ˈdiː]	Personalausweis
current account	[ˈkʌrənt əkaʊnt]	Girokonto
to **deposit money**	[dɪˌpɒzɪt ˈmʌni]	Geld einzahlen
account holder	[əˈkaʊnt həʊldə]	Kontoinhaber/in
debit card	[ˈdebɪt kɑːd]	Geldkarte
cash	[kæʃ]	Bargeld
ATM	[ˌeɪ tiː ˈem]	Geldautomat
(bank) statement	[ˈsteɪtmənt]	Kontoauszug
to **debit money**	[ˌdebɪt ˈmʌni]	Geld abbuchen
to **credit money**	[ˌkredɪt ˈmʌni]	Geld gutschreiben

The English alphabet

a [eɪ]
b [biː]
c [siː]
d [diː]
e [iː]
f [ef]
g [dʒiː]
h [eɪtʃ]
i [aɪ]
j [dʒeɪ]
k [keɪ]
l [el]
m [em]
n [en]
o [əʊ]
p [piː]
q [kjuː]
r [ɑː]
s [es]
t [tiː]
u [juː]
v [viː]
w [ˈdʌbljuː]
x [eks]
y [waɪ]
z [zed]

Alphabetische Wortliste

Dieses Wörterverzeichnis enthält alle Wörter aus Do it! Advanced in alphabetischer Reihenfolge. Wörter, die in den Audiound Videotexten vorkommen, sind mit einem T bzw. einem V und Wörter, die in den *Pairwork files* vorkommen, mit einem P hinter der Seitenzahl gekennzeichnet.

3D printing *47* 3D-Druck

A

acceptable *41* akzeptabel
accommodation *11* Unterkunft
accordingly *26* entsprechend
account, current ~ *78V* Girokonto; **savings ~** *76* Sparkonto; **~ holder** *78V* Kontoinhaber/in
accounts *pl* *36* Buchhaltung
to **act** *26* handeln
action point *23* Maßnahme, Aktionspunkt
ad *49T* Anzeige, Werbespot, Werbung
to **adapt (to sth)** *60* sich (an etw) anpassen, sich an etw gewöhnen
address, proof of ~ *78V* Adressnachweis
administration, business ~ *18* Betriebswirtschaft
advert(isement) *49T* Anzeige, Werbespot, Werbung
to **advertise: ~ sth** *46V, 48* für etw Werbung machen, etw bewerben; **~ a job** *18* eine Stelle ausschreiben
advice, careers ~ *39* Berufsberatung
advisor, careers ~ *11* Berufsberater/in
afraid: ... I'm ~ ... *38T* leider, ich fürchte
agenda *33* Tagesordnung
agent, customer service ~ *35* Kundendienstmitarbeiter/in
agreement *81* Vereinbarung
ahead, straight ~ *37* geradeaus; to **go ~ with sth** *46* etw durchführen, etw machen; **Go ~.** *31* Schieß los! Erzähl mal!
alcoholic *60* Alkoholiker/in
alive *36* lebendig
almost *7* fast, beinahe
alternative *23* andere/r/s, Ausweich-, alternativ
alternative *45* Alternative
amazed, to be ~ at sth *73T* über etw erstaunt sein
amazing *31* toll, unglaublich
amount *46* Menge
to **apologize to sb** *71* sich bei jdm entschuldigen
apology *59* Entschuldigung
appliance *50* Haushaltsgerät, Elektrogerät
applicant *15* Bewerber/in
application *15* Bewerbung; **~ form** *78T* Antragsformular
to **apply for sth** *9V, 9T* sich für/um etw bewerben; *48* etw beantragen
appropriate *41* angemessen, geeignet
Arctic Circle *70V* Polarkreis
area, vocational ~ *15* Berufsfeld
argument, to **have ~s about sth** *29T* sich um etw streiten
arrangement, to **make ~s** *66* Vorbereitungen treffen, Termine ausmachen, Buchungen vornehmen
arrival, new ~ *71* Neuankömmling
artist, tattoo ~ *24* Tätowierer/in
arts and crafts *pl* *17* Basteln, Werken
asleep, to **fall ~** *17* einschlafen
assistant, business ~ *24* kaufmännische/r Assistent/in
at once *38V* sofort
ATM *78V* Geldautomat
to **attach sth** *19P* *(E-Mail:)* etw anhängen
attachment *23* *(E-Mail:)* Anhang
attendant, flight ~ *35* Flugbegleiter/in
attention to detail *16* Detailgenauigkeit, Liebe zum Detail
automatically *51* automatisch
axis *53* Achse

B

baby, to **deliver a ~** *40* ein Kind zur Welt bringen
back, straight ~ *28V* gerader Rücken
bad: Too ~! *43T* Pech gehabt!
bags *pl*, to **check in one's ~** *69T* sein Gepäck aufgeben
to **bake** *6* backen
balance *43T* Kontostand, Saldo
balcony *81* Balkon
bamboo *47* Bambus
ban *46* Verbot
to **ban sth** *46* etw verbieten
bank: ~ balance *43T* Kontostand, Saldo; **~ statement** *78V* Kontoauszug; **~ transfer** *78T* Überweisung
banking *78* Bankgeschäfte
bar chart *14* Säulendiagramm
battery *41* Akku, Batterie
to **be: ~ off sick** *73T* krankgeschrieben sein; **~ up to sth** *11* etw vorhaben, etw machen, etw anstellen; **If I were you ...** *46* an deiner/Ihrer Stelle
to **behave** *17* sich benehmen
to **belong somewhere** *41* wohin gehören
bench *59* Bank
bilingual *18* zweisprachig
billion *47* Milliarde
bin, rubbish ~ *51* Abfalleimer, Mülltonne
birdwatching *21* Vogelbeobachtung
biscuit *33T* Keks
blood *30* Blut
boarding pass *69T* Bordkarte
boatyard *40* Bootswerft
bold *62* fettgedruckt
border *70V* Grenze
to **borrow sth** *76* sich etw leihen
bottled *46V* in Flaschen
bowl *60* Schale, Schüssel
brake *65* Bremse
branch *78V* Filiale, Zweigstelle
to **break** *55* kaputtgehen; **~ the ice** *12* das Eis brechen
to **breathe** *8* atmen, durchatmen
brief *26* kurz
brochure *57* Prospekt
to **brush one's teeth** *50* sich die Zähne putzen
budget *79* Haushalt, Budget, Etat
to **budget sth** *76* sich etw *(Geld usw.)* einteilen, mit etw sparsam umgehen
budgeting *79* Haushaltsplanung, Finanzplanung
bulb, LED ~ *51P* LED-Leuchte, LED; **light ~** *50* Glühbirne
to **burn sth** *78T* etw verbrennen
business: ~ administration *18* Betriebswirtschaft; **~ assistant** *24* kaufmännische/r Assistent/in; **~ card** *13* (geschäftliche) Visitenkarte; **~ training** *15* kaufmännische Ausbildung
by the hour *6* stundenweise, pro Stunde

C

to **calculate sth** *46* etw berechnen, etw ausrechnen
call, to **take a ~** *40* einen Anruf entgegennehmen
camera operator *34* Kameramann/-frau
to **camp** *70V* zelten
campaign *49T* Kampagne, Aktion
to **canoe** *70(V)* mit dem Kanu fahren
canteen *35* Kantine
capital *71* Hauptstadt
capsule *46* Kapsel
captain *15* Kapitän/in
car, used ~ *76* Gebrauchtwagen

card, business ~ *13* (geschäftliche) Visitenkarte; **debit** ~ *78V* Geldkarte; **door entry** ~ *37* Zugangskarte
care, health ~ *5* Gesundheitswesen, Gesundheitsfürsorge; **home** ~ *40* häusliche Krankenpflege; **social** ~ *5* Sozialwesen, Sozialfürsorge; **Take ~!** *6* Pass auf dich auf! Mach's gut!
to **care: sb ~es about sth** *46* jdm liegt etw am Herzen
career: ~s advice *39* Berufsberatung; **~s advisor** *11* Berufsberater/in
carpenter *24* Schreiner/in, Tischler/in
to **carry sth out** *48* etw durchführen, etw in die Tat umsetzen
cash *78V* Bargeld; to **pay** ~ *76* bar zahlen
casual *26* *(Kleidung:)* leger, salopp
to **catch:** ~ **sth** *58* etw kriegen, etw erwischen; to **get caught in sth** *70V* in etw stecken bleiben
category *79* Rubrik, Kategorie, Gruppe
catering *15* Gastronomie
to **cause sth** *16* etw verursachen
to celebrate *11* feiern; ~ **in style** *78T* groß feiern
century *51* Jahrhundert
to **change** *16* sich verändern
change *78T* Wechselgeld; **climate** ~ *50* Klimawandel
to **change one's clothes** *31* sich umziehen
charge *68* Gebühr
to **charge a fee** *78V* eine Gebühr verlangen
chart, pie ~ *14* Tortendiagramm
to **check:** ~ **out** *68* abreisen, auschecken; ~ **in one's bags** *69T* sein Gepäck aufgeben
check-up, medical ~ *23* ärztliche Untersuchung; to **give sb a** ~ *40* jdn untersuchen
childcare *15* Kinderbetreuung
chocolate maker *44* Chocolatier/-ière
choice *6* Wahl
circle, Arctic C~ *70V* Polarkreis
class, special ~ *56* Förderkurs
to **clear a table** *20P* den Tisch abräumen
climate change *50* Klimawandel
to **climb** *52* steigen, nach oben klettern
closely, to look at sth *20V, 76* sich etw genau ansehen
cloth *51* Stoff, Tuch
clothes *pl*, to **change one's** ~ *31* sich umziehen
coconut *45* Kokosnuss
coding *19* Programmierung
to **collect sth** *46V, 73T* etw sammeln
collection, waste ~ *46* Müllabfuhr
coloured *31* farbig, bunt
company, pharmaceutical ~ *42T* Pharmaunternehmen; to **start a** ~ *10* ein Unternehmen gründen
competition *53* (die) Konkurrenz; *70* Wettbewerb
competitor *71* Konkurrent/in
complaint *58* Beschwerde, Reklamation, Klage
computing *5* Datenverarbeitung
conclusions *pl* *33T* Fazit
to **connect to sth** *48* eine emotionale Verbindung zu etw herstellen
construction *15* Baugewerbe
consumer *49T* Verbraucher/in
to **contact sb** *22* sich mit jdm in Verbindung setzen
container *46V, 50* Gefäß, Behälter
contract *29T* Vertrag
contribution *54* Beitrag
to **convince sb of sth** *49T* jdn von etw überzeugen
cooler, water ~ *46* Trinkwasserspender
corridor *36* Flur, Gang
cosmetics *pl* *53P* Kosmetik(artikel)
course, training ~ *13* Schulung
to **cover sth** *14* etw *(Thema usw.)* behandeln; *80* etw *(Kosten usw.)* decken
crafts *pl*, **arts and** ~ *17* Basteln, Werken
to **credit money** *78V* Geld gutschreiben
cultural *60* kulturell
culture *30T* Kultur
currency exchange *78T* Geldumtausch, Währungsumtausch
current account *78V* Girokonto
customer service agent *35* Kundendienstmitarbeiter/in
to **cut sth** *46V* etw vermeiden, etw senken
cyber security *16* Cybersicherheit
to **cycle** *17* radeln

D

damaged *55* beschädigt
date, expiry ~ *78T* Ablaufdatum; to **keep sth up to** ~ *18* etw auf dem neuesten Stand halten
day, open ~ *43* Tag der offenen Tür
dead *59* tot
to **deal with sth** *53* sich mit etw beschäftigen, etw zum Gegenstand haben; *78* mit etw umgehen
debit card *78V* Geldkarte
to **debit money** *78V* Geld abbuchen
debts *pl* *79* Schulden
decision, final ~ *46* endgültige Entscheidung
to **decrease** *52* abnehmen, sinken
delay *69T* Verspätung, Verzögerung
delay *28V* Verzögerung
to **deliver:** ~ **sth** *55* etw liefern, etw zustellen; ~ **a baby** *40* ein Kind zur Welt bringen
to **depart** *74* abreisen
department *6* Abteilung
depending on sth *62* je nachdem …, abhängig von etw
deposit *81* Kaution
to **deposit money** *78V* Geld einzahlen
design *6* Konstruktion, Design; *14* Gestaltung, Layout
to **design:** to **be ~ed for sb/sth** *62* für jdn/etw gedacht sein, sich an jdn/etw richten
detail, attention to ~ *16* Detailgenauigkeit, Liebe zum Detail
to **develop sth** *16* etw entwickeln
development, product ~ *36* Produktentwicklung
diamond *70V* Diamant
diary *65T* Kalender
diet *54* Ernährung, Kost
digit *78T* Ziffer
diploma *18* Diplom, Abschlusszeugnis
discovery *17* Entdeckung
dish *60* *(Essen:)* Gericht
disorganized *43* unorganisiert, schlecht organisiert
disrespectful *61* respektlos
to **divide sth into sth** *14* etw in etw aufteilen
dog: ~ **sled** *70V* Hundeschlitten; ~ **team** *70* Hundegespann
door entry card *37* Zugangskarte
doorstep, on one's ~ *70* vor der (eigenen) Tür
dos and don'ts *pl* *26* *Dinge, die man tun bzw. lassen sollte*
dramatical(ly) *52T* dramatisch
to **dress informally** *41* sich leger kleiden
drive *40* Autofahrt
to **drop** *52* fallen
to **dry** *62* trocknen
duty, to **go off** ~ *68* Dienstschluss haben

E

eating out *79* essen gehen
education *10* Bildung, Ausbildung, Lernen; **further** ~ *20P* Weiterbildung
electrician, marine ~ *40* Schiffselektriker/in
electrics *40* Elektrik

electronics *40* Elektronik
emergency fund *76* Notfallfonds, Rücklagen für Notfälle
to **enclose sth** *18* *(Brief:)* etw beifügen
to **entertain sb** *74* jdn bewirten, jdn unterhalten
entry, door ~ card *37* Zugangskarte
environmental label *48* Umweltsiegel
especially *6* besonders, insbesondere
to **estimate sth** *84* etw schätzen
exchange, currency ~ *78T* Geldumtausch, Währungsumtausch; **~ rate** *78T* Wechselkurs
excited, to **feel ~ about sth** *9T* von etw begeistert sein
expenses *pl* *79* Ausgaben; **travel ~** *23* Reisekosten
to **experience sth** *6* etw erfahren, etw erleben
expiry date *78T* Ablaufdatum
extract *43* Auszug, Ausschnitt
extrovert, to **be an ~** *20V* extrovertiert sein

F

face-to-face *28V* persönlich
fact-finding *73T* Erkundung
factory *7* Fabrik
fair, trade ~ *66* Messe, Fachmesse, Branchenmesse
familiar, to **be ~ with sth** *19* mit etw vertraut sein, sich mit etw auskennen
family, sense of ~ *81* familiäres Miteinander
to **fall asleep** *17* einschlafen
fascinated *43T* fasziniert
fee, rebooking ~ *69T* Umbuchungsgebühr; to **charge a ~** *78V* eine Gebühr verlangen
to **feel excited about sth** *9T* von etw begeistert sein
festival *31* Fest, Festtag
figures *pl*, **sales ~** *52* Verkaufszahlen, Umsatzzahlen
file *18* Datei, Aktenordner
to **fill in a form** *6* ein Formular ausfüllen
final decision *46* endgültige Entscheidung
to **finance sth** *75* etw finanzieren
financial planning *76* Finanzplanung
firefighter *15* Feuerwehrmann/-frau
first floor *AE* *37* Erdgeschoss
to **fish** *70V* angeln
to **fix sth** *58V* etw reparieren
flag, national ~ *71* Nationalflagge
flat, to **share a ~ with sb** *80* mit jdm zusammenwohnen
flight attendant *35* Flugbegleiter/in
floor, first ~ *AE* *37* Erdgeschoss; **ground ~** *BE* *37* Erdgeschoss; **~ plan** *36* Grundriss, Raumplan
flour *45* Mehl
to **fly in** *66* *(mit dem Flugzeug)* ankommen
focus (on sth) *18* Schwerpunkt (auf etw)
to **follow up** *58V* nachfassen
follow-up *40* Nachbereitung, Nachfassen
food, leftover ~ *50* Essensreste
for now *42T* einstweilen, erst einmal
form, application ~ *78T* Antragsformular; to **fill in a ~** *6* ein Formular ausfüllen
frozen lake *71* zugefrorener See
fruit, to **pick ~** *11* Obst pflücken, Obst ernten
frustrated *10* frustriert
fully furnished *80* komplett möbliert
fun *17* lustig, spaßig
fund, emergency ~ *76* Notfallfonds, Rücklagen für Notfälle
furnished, fully ~ *80* komplett möbliert
further *18* weiter; **~ education** *20P* Weiterbildung

G

gardener, landscape ~ *24* Landschaftsgärtner/in
gate *69T* Flugsteig, Gate
genuinely *48* wirklich, ernsthaft
to **get: ~ caught in sth** *70V* in etw stecken bleiben; **~ used to sth** *80* sich an etw gewöhnen
to **give sb a check-up** *40* jdn untersuchen
glacier *70(V)* Gletscher
global leader *18* Weltmarktführer
to **go: ~ ahead with sth** *46* etw durchführen, etw machen; **Go ahead.** *31* Schieß los! Erzähl mal! **~ off duty** *68* Dienstschluss haben; **~ sledding** *70* mit dem Hundeschlitten fahren; to **keep sth going** *31* etw am Laufen halten
to **graduate** *10* den (Uni-/Schul-) Abschluss machen
graph, line ~ *52* Liniendiagramm, Kurvendiagramm
greenhouse gases *pl* *50* Treibhausgase
greeting *26* Begrüßung; **~s** *pl* *11* Grüße
grid *83* Raster
ground floor *BE* *37* Erdgeschoss
to **grow** *18* wachsen
to **guess: I never ~ed.** *31* Das hätte ich nie gedacht. Darauf wäre ich nie gekommen.
guideline *41* Vorgabe, Richtlinie, Hinweis

H

habit *46(V)* Gewohnheit
hairdryer *62* Föhn
to **handle sb/sth** *58V* mit jdm/etw umgehen
to **hang on a minute** *62* kurz warten
happiness *54* Glück, Zufriedenheit
harbour *20P* Hafen
hard, to **look ~ at sb/sth** *20V* jdn/etw genau unter die Lupe nehmen; to **try ~** *79* sich (große) Mühe geben; **sb has a ~ time doing sth** *60* jdm fällt es schwer, etw zu tun
to **have: ~ arguments about sth** *29T* sich um etw streiten; **~ sth lined up** *28* etw vorhaben, etw geplant haben
head, to **nod the ~** *61* mit dem Kopf nicken; to **hit one's ~ on sth** *81* sich den Kopf an etw stoßen; **~ office** *18* Zentrale, Firmensitz
health: ~ care *5* Gesundheitswesen, Gesundheitsfürsorge; **~ and safety** *29T* Arbeitssicherheit
heating *84* Heizung
to **highlight sth** *48* etw hervorheben
highly, to **be ~ likely** *9T* sehr wahrscheinlich sein; **~-qualified** *8* hochqualifiziert
to **hire sb** *75* jdn engagieren
to **hit one's head on sth** *81* sich den Kopf an etw stoßen
holiday, working ~ *20P* Arbeitsurlaub
home care *40* häusliche Krankenpflege
horse riding *5* Reiten
hour, by the ~ *6* stundenweise, pro Stunde; to **work long ~s** *16* lange arbeiten, Überstunden machen
housekeeper *68* *(Hotel:)* Reinigungskraft
HR manager *18* Personalleiter/in, Personalsachbearbeiter/in
human resources (HR) *pl* *6* Personal(abteilung)
hunter, whale ~ *70* Walfänger/in

I

ice, to **break the ~** *12* das Eis brechen
ID *78V* Personalausweis
i.e. (= that is) *83* d.h. (= das heißt, nämlich)
idea: I have no ~. *14* Ich habe keine Ahnung.

If I were you ... *46* an deiner/Ihrer Stelle
to **imagine sth** *9T* sich etw vorstellen
immigrant *56* Einwanderer/-in
to **immigrate** *70* einwandern
immigration *69T* Passkontrolle; *71* Einwanderung; **~ officer** *35* Grenzbeamte/r, Beamte/r bei der Einreisekontrolle
impact *52T* Auswirkung(en), Folge(n)
impression, to **make an ~** *26* einen Eindruck hinterlassen
income *11* Einkommen
to **increase** *52* steigen, zunehmen
incredible *31* unglaublich
industry *9V, 48* Branche
informally, to **dress ~** *41* sich leger kleiden
innovation *72* Neuerung, Innovation
to **inspire sb to do sth** *46V* jdn dazu anregen, etw zu tun
insulting *61* beleidigend
insurance *40* Versicherung
interest *78V* Zins(en)
intern *9* Praktikant/in
internship *6* Praktikum
to **interview for sth** *43T* Vorstellungsgespräche für etw führen
introvert, to **be an ~** *20V* introvertiert sein
invention *72* Erfindung
to **invest** *48* investieren

J

jam jar *50* Marmeladenglas
job, permanent ~ *16* unbefristete Stelle, Festanstellung; **summer ~** *9V, 43* Ferienjob
jobseeker *40* Arbeitssuchende/r
to **join: May I ~ you?** *12* Darf ich mich zu Ihnen gesellen/setzen?
journey *10* Reise, Weg; **return ~** *68* Rückfahrt

K

to **keep: ~ in touch with sb** *6* mit jdm in Verbindung bleiben; **~ sth up to date** *18* etw auf dem neuesten Stand halten; **~ sb waiting** *38V* jdn warten lassen; **~ sth going** *31* etw am Laufen halten
key *21* wichtig, entscheidend, Haupt-
keyword *21* Stichwort

L

label, environmental ~ *48* Umweltsiegel
lake, frozen ~ *71* zugefrorener See
landfill *50* Mülldeponie
landlord *81* Vermieter
landscape gardener *24* Landschaftsgärtner/in
laundry, to **do the ~** *40* Wäsche waschen
leader *15* Führungspersönlichkeit; **global ~** *18* Weltmarktführer
to **learn: ~ sth** *22* etw erfahren; **~ about sth** *9* etw über etw in Erfahrung bringen
LED bulb *51P* LED-Leuchte, LED
leftover food *50* Essensreste
lid *45* Deckel
life, professional ~ *25* Berufsleben
lift *81* Aufzug, Fahrstuhl
light, Northern L~s *pl 70V* Polarlicht, Nordlicht; **~ bulb** *50* Glühbirne
likely, to **be highly ~** *9T* sehr wahrscheinlich sein
line *69T* Leitung, Verbindung; **~ graph** *52* Liniendiagramm, Kurvendiagramm
lined up, to **have sth ~** *28* etw vorhaben, etw geplant haben
link *28* Bindeglied, Verbindung
liveable *71* lebenswert
loan *77* Kredit
to **log into sth** *40* sich in etw einloggen
long, in the ~ run *50* langfristig, auf lange Sicht; to **work ~ hours** *16* lange arbeiten, Überstunden machen; **~-term** *76* langfristig
to **look: ~ after sth** *28* sich um etw kümmern; **~ closely at sth** *20V, 76* sich etw genau ansehen; **~ hard at sb/sth** *20V* jdn/etw genau unter die Lupe nehmen
loose *50* lose, unverpackt
lorry *BE 36* Lastwagen, Lkw
luck: Best of ~! *36* Alles Gute! Viel Glück!
lucky number *60* Glückszahl

M

to **make: ~ an impression** *26* einen Eindruck hinterlassen; **~ sense** *29T* einleuchten, vernünftig sein; **~ arrangements** *66* Vorbereitungen treffen, Termine ausmachen, Buchungen vornehmen
to **manage sth** *10* etw verwalten, mit etw umgehen
management *81* Verwaltung
manager *81* Verwalter/in; **HR ~** *18* Personalleiter/in, Personalsachbearbeiter/in; **sales ~** *36* Vertriebsleiter/in
maple syrup *71* Ahornsirup
marine electrician *40* Schiffselektriker/in
to **market sth** *48* etw vermarkten
marketer *49T* Vermarkter/in, Marketingfachmann/-frau
marketing *36* Vermarktung, Marketing
May I join you? *12* Darf ich mich zu Ihnen gesellen/setzen?
to **mediate** *63* vermitteln
medical: ~ check-up *23* ärztliche Untersuchung; **~ technician** *35* Medizintechniker/in
meditating *40* Meditieren
to **meet requirements** *19P* Voraussetzungen erfüllen
mentor *8* Mentor/in
mess, to **be a ~** *25* unordentlich sein, schlampig sein
message, voice ~ *51* Sprachnachricht
to **message sb** *66* jdm eine Nachricht schicken, sich bei jdm melden
messy *14* chaotisch, unübersichtlich
million, never in a ~ years *31* nie im Leben
to **mind** *28* etw dagegen haben
minute, to **hang on a ~** *62* kurz warten
minutes *pl 72* Protokoll
misunderstanding *60* Missverständnis
module *48* Modul
moment, present ~ *10* Augenblick
money, to **credit ~** *78V* Geld gutschreiben; to **debit ~** *78V* Geld abbuchen; to **deposit ~** *78V* Geld einzahlen

N

name tag *13* Namensschild
national flag *71* Nationalflagge
neat and tidy *26* sauber und ordentlich
needs *pl 16* Bedürfnisse
net *84* netto
network *16* Netzwerk, Netz
never in a million years *31* nie im Leben
new arrival *71* Neuankömmling
to **nod the head** *61* mit dem Kopf nicken
Northern Lights *pl 70V* Polarlicht, Nordlicht
now, for ~ *42T* einstweilen, erst einmal
number, lucky ~ *60* Glückszahl

O

obviously *49T* natürlich
off, to **be ~ sick** *73T* krankgeschrieben sein; to **go ~ duty** *68* Dienstschluss haben
to **offend sb** *61* jdn kränken, jdn beleidigen

office, head ~ *18* Zentrale, Firmensitz
officer, immigration ~ *35* Grenzbeamte/r, Beamte/r bei der Einreisekontrolle
OK, to **work out ~** *43T* sich von alleine regeln/erledigen
once, at ~ *38V* sofort
open day *43* Tag der offenen Tür
operator, camera ~ *34* Kameramann/-frau
optician *24* Optiker/in
organic *48* Bio-
organization *6* (größeres) Unternehmen
organizational *18* organisatorisch, Organisations-
organized *15* (gut) organisiert
ought: sb ~ to do sth *25* jd sollte etw tun
outline *43T* Gliederung, Entwurf
overdraft *10* Kontoüberziehung, Dispo, Minus
to **overreact** *63* überreagieren
overtime *83* Überstunden

P

to **package sth** *18* etw verpacken
packaging *6* Verpackung
packet *50* Packung
packing *36* Verpackung
panel, solar ~ *40* Solarmodul
parking space *81* Parkplatz
part, spare ~ *40* Ersatzteil
participant *32* Teilnehmer/in
to **pause** *28V* warten, pausieren
to **pay: ~ cash** *76* bar zahlen; **~ sb/sth a visit** *67* jdm/etw einen Besuch abstatten
peace *30T* Frieden
period, trial ~ *38* Probezeit
permanent job *16* unbefristete Stelle, Festanstellung
person, private ~ *30T* zurückhaltender Mensch
petrol *76* Benzin
pharmaceutical company *42T* Pharmaunternehmen
to **pick: ~ sb/sth up** *37* jdn/etw abholen; **~ sth up** *51* etw aufheben; **~ fruit** *11* Obst pflücken, Obst ernten
pie chart *14* Tortendiagramm
place, to **take ~** *57* stattfinden
plain *41* einfarbig, schlicht
plan, floor ~ *36* Grundriss, Raumplan
planning, financial ~ *76* Finanzplanung
plant *42T* Werk, Fabrik
plate *61* Teller
playground *17* Spielplatz
plenty of *66* viel, genügend
point, action ~ *23* Maßnahme, Aktionspunkt; **What's the ~ of ...?** *58V* Welchen Sinn hat ...? **I see your ~.** *54* Ich verstehe, worauf Sie hinauswollen.
pollution *46* Verschmutzung
population *70V* Bevölkerung
powder *31* Pulver
prairie *70* Steppe, Prärie
to **prepare sth** *14* etw *(Text usw.)* erstellen
present moment *10* Augenblick
previous *52T* vorig, vorhergehend
printing, 3D ~ *47* 3D-Druck
printout *28V* Ausdruck
private person *30T* zurückhaltender Mensch
producer *70V* Produzent/in
product development *36* Produktentwicklung
production plant *42T* Werk, Fabrik
professional life *25* Berufsleben
to **promise** *49T* versprechen
proof of address *78V* Adressnachweis
province *70* Provinz
punctual *60* pünktlich
to **push in** *55* sich vordrängeln

Q

qualified, highly-~ *8* hochqualifiziert
to **qualify** *18* den/seinen Abschluss machen
quarter *52T* Quartal
to **quit** *39* kündigen
quote *10* Zitat

R

to **rate sth** *64* etw bewerten
rate, exchange ~ *78T* Wechselkurs
rating *64* Bewertung
to **realize: sb ~ed sth** *81* jdm wird etw klar
rebooking fee *69T* Umbuchungsgebühr
recently *20P* vor kurzem
reception *5* Empfang, Rezeption
receptionist *35* Empfangsmitarbeiter/in, Rezeptionist/in
recipe *36* Rezept
records *pl* *18* Datensätze, Akten
recyclable *50* wiederverwertbar, recyclebar
to **refer back to sth** *73T* auf etw zurückkommen
reference *9V, 18* Referenz
to **refuse sth** *61* etw ablehnen
to **register** *11* sich anmelden
regular *80* normal
relevant, to **be ~ to sth** *21T* einen Bezug zu etw haben, mit etw zu tun haben
rent *79* Miete
repair *20P* Reparatur
reputation *46* Ruf
request, on ~ *20P* auf Anfrage
to **require sth** *19P* etw erfordern, etw benötigen
requirement, to **meet ~s** *19P* Voraussetzungen erfüllen
result, as a ~ *42T* folglich, infolgedessen
retired *56* im Ruhestand, pensioniert
return journey *68* Rückfahrt
reusable *46* wiederverwendbar
review *81* Kritik, Rezension, Besprechung
to **review sth** *56* etw erneut prüfen, etw überprüfen
to **rewrite sth** *33* etw umformulieren, etw neu schreiben
riding, horse ~ *5* Reiten
to **rise** *52* ansteigen
risky *41* riskant, gefährlich
roommate *81* Mitbewohner/in
route *38V* Strecke
rubbish bin *51* Abfalleimer, Mülltonne
run, in the long ~ *50* langfristig, auf lange Sicht
rush, to **be in a ~** *36* in Eile sein, es eilig haben

S

safety, health and ~ *29T* Arbeitssicherheit
salary *19* Gehalt; **starting ~** *29T* Einstiegsgehalt, Anfangsgehalt
sales *pl* *6* Vertrieb, Verkauf; *42T* Umsatz; **~ figures** *pl* *52* Verkaufszahlen, Umsatzzahlen; **~ manager** *36* Vertriebsleiter/in
satisfaction *11* Zufriedenheit
savings *pl* *79* Ersparnisse; **~ account** *76* Sparkonto
saw *35* Säge
school, summer ~ *14* Ferienkurs(e)
scriptwriter *34* Drehbuchautor/in
season, to **be in ~** *50* Saison haben
seat *69T* Platz, Sitz; **Have a ~.** *38T* Nehmen Sie Platz!
security *69T (Flughafen usw.:)* Sicherheitskontrolle; **cyber ~** *16* Cybersicherheit
sell-by date *50* Haltbarkeitsdatum
sense: ~ of family *81* familiäres Miteinander; to **make ~** *29T* einleuchten, vernünftig sein
to **separate sth** *60* etw trennen
serious *21T* ernstzunehmend
seriously *31* im Ernst; to **take sth ~** *26* etw ernst nehmen
service *58V, 61* Dienstleistung; *65T* Wartung, Inspektion; **customer ~ agent** *35* Kundendienstmitarbeiter/in

to **service sth** *6* etw warten, etw instandhalten
to **share: ~ sth with sb** *84* sich etw mit jdm teilen; **~ (a flat) with sb** *80* mit jdm zusammenwohnen
shared *80* gemeinsam (genutzt)
shift *40* Schicht
shiny *76* glänzend, blitzblank
shipping *36* Versand
shopper *54* Kunde/Kundin *(im Einzelhandel)*
short, to **be ~ of sth** *38T* zu wenig(e) von etw haben
to **shout at sb** *31* jdn anschreien
to **show sb around** *36* jdn herumführen
sick, to **be off ~** *73T* krankgeschrieben sein
to **sign sth** *37* etw unterzeichnen
silence *30* Stille
single-use *46* Einweg-
to **sit up straight** *26* gerade sitzen
to **skip sth** *41* etw auslassen, auf etw verzichten
sled, dog ~ *70V* Hundeschlitten
sledding, to **go ~** *70* mit dem Hundeschlitten fahren
smell *58V* Geruch, Gestank
smile, to **be all ~s** *36* über das ganze Gesicht strahlen
soap *45* Seife
social care *5* Sozialwesen, Sozialfürsorge
to **socialize** *13* sich (privat) mit Leuten treffen
solar panel *40* Solarmodul
to **sort sth into sth** *47* etw nach etw sortieren
spanner *35* Schraubenschlüssel
spare: ~ part *40* Ersatzteil; **~ time** *48* Freizeit
special class *56* Förderkurs
to **specialize in sth** *29T* sich auf etw spezialisieren
specifications *pl* *72* technische Daten
spectacular *70V* atemberaubend, spektakulär
spicy *66* pikant, würzig, scharf
stain *41* Schmutzfleck
stamp *35* Stempel
to **stand up** *59* aufstehen
to **start a company** *10* ein Unternehmen gründen
starting salary *29T* Einstiegsgehalt, Anfangsgehalt
to **state** *57* sagen, angeben, behaupten
statement *78V* Kontoauszug
to **stay with sb** *68* bei jdm übernachten
stick *45* Stab
to **stir sth** *45* etw umrühren
straight: ~ ahead *37* geradeaus; **~ back** *28V* gerader Rücken; to **sit up ~** *26* gerade sitzen
stranger *13* Fremde/r, Unbekannte/r
straw *46* Strohhalm
strict *61* streng
a strong swimmer *11P* ein/e gute/r Schwimmer/in
structure *14* Aufbau, Struktur
structured, well-~ *14* übersichtlich aufgebaut, gut strukturiert
style, to celebrate in ~ *78T* groß feiern
suit *8* Anzug
summer: ~ job *9V, 43* Ferienjob; **~ school** *14* Ferienkurs(e)
support *16* Hilfe, Unterstützung
to **support: ~ sb/sth** *18* jdn/etw unterstützen; **~ sth** *54* etw *(Argument usw.)* untermauern, etw stärken
suspicious, to **be ~ of sth** *48* einer Sache gegenüber misstrauisch sein
to **switch sth on** *51P* etw einschalten
swimmer, a strong ~ *11P* ein/e gute/r Schwimmer/in
syringe *35* Spritze
syrup, maple ~ *71* Ahornsirup

T

table, to **clear a ~** *20P* den Tisch abräumen
tag, name ~ *13* Namensschild
to **take: ~ sth seriously** *26* etw ernst nehmen; **~ place** *57* stattfinden; **T~ care!** *6* Pass auf dich auf! Mach's gut! **T~ your time.** *29T* Lassen Sie sich Zeit! **~ a call** *40* einen Anruf entgegennehmen
takeaway *46* *(Essen:)* zum Mitnehmen
talk *46* Vortrag
tap *51* Wasserhahn; **~ water** *46* Leitungswasser
tasty *36* lecker
tattoo artist *24* Tätowierer/in
team, dog ~ *70* Hundegespann
technical training *15* technische Ausbildung
technician, medical ~ *35* Medizintechniker/in
technique *48* Methode, Technik
term, long-~ *76* langfristig
territory *70* Gebiet
to **test sth** *16* etw prüfen, etw testen
to **throw sth at sb** *31* jdn mit etw bewerfen
thumb *61* Daumen
to **tick sth** *83* etw abhaken, etw mit einem Häkchen versehen
tidy, neat and ~ *26* sauber und ordentlich
tight *41* *(Kleidung:)* enganliegend, knapp
time, spare ~ *48* Freizeit; **sb has a hard ~ doing sth** *60* jdm fällt es schwer, etw zu tun; **Take your ~.** *29T* Lassen Sie sich Zeit!
timetable *38V* Fahrplan
tip *61* Trinkgeld
tired, to **be ~ of sth** *76* etw leid sein, etw satthaben
Too bad! *43T* Pech gehabt!
tooth: to **brush one's teeth** *50* sich die Zähne putzen
total *53* Gesamt-
touch, to **keep in ~ with sb** *6* mit jdm in Verbindung bleiben
trade fair *66* Messe, Fachmesse, Branchenmesse
to **train as a …** *8* eine Ausbildung zum … machen
training, business ~ *15* kaufmännische Ausbildung; **technical ~** *15* technische Ausbildung; **~ course** *13* Schulung
to **translate** *6* übersetzen
to **transport sth** *6* etw befördern, etw transportieren
travel expenses *pl* *23* Reisekosten
trial period *38* Probezeit
trillion *47* Billion
truth *29* Wahrheit
to **try hard** *79* sich (große) Mühe geben

U

uneducated *10* ungebildet, schlecht ausgebildet
unfurnished *81* unmöbliert
uniform *35* Dienstkleidung, Uniform
unprepared *43* unvorbereitet
untidy *25* unaufgeräumt, unordentlich
up, to **be ~ to sth** *11* etw vorhaben, etw machen, etw anstellen; **What's ~?** *8* Was gibt's?; to **keep sth ~ to date** *18* etw auf dem neuesten Stand halten
to **update sth** *16* etw aktualisieren, etw updaten
use, single-~ *46* Einweg-
to **use:** to **get used to sth** *80* sich an etw gewöhnen
used car *76* Gebrauchtwagen
utilities *pl* *80* Nebenkosten

V

view *36* Aussicht
virtual *81* virtuell
visit, to **pay sb/sth a ~** *67* jdm/etw einen Besuch abstatten
vocational area *15* Berufsfeld

voice message *51* Sprachnachricht
volume *28V* Lautstärke

W

to **wait:** to **keep sb waiting** *38V* jdn warten lassen
to **walk past sth** *51* an etw vorbeilaufen
wants *pl 79* Wünsche
warehouse *40* Lager
washable *46V* waschbar
waste collection *46* Müllabfuhr
water, tap ~ *46* Leitungswasser; **~ cooler** *46* Trinkwasserspender
watermaker *40* Wasseraufbereitungsanlage, Entsalzer
well-structured *14* übersichtlich aufgebaut, gut strukturiert
whale hunter *70* Walfänger/in
whole, as a ~ *48* als Ganzes
wilderness *70V* Wildnis
within *71* innerhalb von
wooden *46* aus Holz
to **work: ~ out** *68* laufen, sich ergeben; **~ out OK** *43T* sich von alleine regeln/erledigen; **~ long hours** *16* lange arbeiten, Überstunden machen
working holiday *20P* Arbeitsurlaub
worth *50* wert
writing, in ~ *81* schriftlich

Y

year, never in a million ~s *31* nie im Leben
yet *65T* schon

Irregular verbs

be	was/were	been	*sein*
break	broke	broken	*brechen, kaputt machen*
bring	brought	brought	*bringen*
buy	bought	bought	*kaufen*
choose	chose	chosen	*wählen*
come	came	come	*kommen*
cost	cost	cost	*kosten*
cut	cut	cut	*schneiden*
do	did	done	*tun, machen*
draw	drew	drawn	*zeichen*
drink	drank	drunk	*trinken*
drive	drove	driven	*fahren*
eat	ate	eaten	*essen*
feel	felt	felt	*fühlen*
fight	fought	fought	*(be)kämpfen*
find	found	found	*finden*
forget	forgot	forgotten	*vergessen*
get	got	got	*bekommen*
give	gave	given	*geben*
go	went	gone	*gehen*
hurt	hurt	hurt	*(sich) verletzen*
know	knew	known	*wissen, kennen*
leave	left	left	*(ver)lassen*
lose	lost	lost	*verlieren*
make	made	made	*machen, tun*
meet	met	met	*treffen*
put	put	put	*legen, stellen, setzen*
read	read	read	*lesen*
ride	rode	ridden	*fahren*
run	ran	run	*laufen, rennen*
say	said	said	*sagen*
see	saw	seen	*sehen*
send	sent	sent	*senden*
show	showed	shown	*zeigen*
sing	sang	sung	*singen*
speak	spoke	spoken	*sprechen*
spend	spent	spent	*ausgeben, verbringen*
steal	stole	stolen	*stehlen*
sweep	swept	swept	*fegen*
take	took	taken	*nehmen*
tell	told	told	*erzählen*
think	thought	thought	*denken*
understand	understood	understood	*verstehen*
wake up	woke up	woken up	*aufwachen*
win	won	won	*gewinnen*
write	wrote	written	*schreiben*

Canada

ARCTIC OCEAN
U.S.
Yukon River
BEAUFORT SEA
Banks Island
Queen Elizabeth Islands
Ellesmere Island
Alert
GREENLAND (DENMARK)
ICELAND
REYKJAVIK
Kaujuitoq (Resolute)
Baffin Bay
Denmark Strait
Inuvik
Dawson
Victoria Island
Cambridge Bay
Baffin Island
Great Bear Lake
Mackenzie River
Echo Bay
Nuuk
Whitehorse
Davis Strait
Watson-Lake
Iqaluit (Frobisher Bay)
Great Slave Lake
Yellowknife
Fort Nelson
Hay River
Fort Smith
Kangiqcliniq (Rankin Inlet)
Ivujivik
LABRADOR SEA
Prince Rupert
Lake Athabasca
Graham Island
Peace River
CANADA
Hudson Bay
Churchill
Prince George
Reindeer Lake
Schefferville
Island of Newfoundland
Happy Valley Goose Bay
Vancouver Island
Edmonton
Saskatchewan River
Nelson River
Gander
Victoria
Vancouver
Flin Flon
Chisasibi (Fort George)
St. John's
Calgary
Saskatoon
Lake Winnipeg
Sept-Îles
Lethbridge
Columbia River
Regina
Moosonee
Chibougamau
Gulf of St. Lawrence
St. Pierre and Miquelon (FRANCE)
Charlottetown
Winnipeg
Thunder Bay
Québec
Fredericton
Halifax
Saint John
Sherbrooke
Snake River
Sudbury
Montréal
Lake Superior
OTTAWA
UNITED STATES
Lake Huron
Lake Ontario
NORTH ATLANTIC OCEAN
Toronto
Missouri River
Mississippi R.
Lake Michigan
London
Hamilton
Windsor
Lake Erie
0 200 400 km
0 200 400 mi

The British Isles

Grammar summary

Word order

G

Subjekt + Verb + Objekt	Ort + Zeit	Adverb + Verb
I enjoy my job.	*We went **to the UK** **last year**.*	*They **often** **chat**.*
Do ***you like your work?***	*Did you meet **on a farm** **in May**?*	*Mia **almost** **forgot**.*
		Aber nach *to be*:
		*It **is usually** on a Sunday.*

Simple present / Simple past

G

Simple present		Simple past	
I/you/we/they work.	He/she/it work**s**.	I/you/he/she/it/we/they work**ed**.	
Do you work?	Do**es** he work?	Did you work?	**Did** he work?
You don't work.	He do**es**n't work.	You didn't work.	He **didn't** work.

Adjectives …

G

machen Ihre Texte interessanter.
Man steigert sie mit *-er/-est* oder *more/most*.

> **!**
> I have a job and ten colleagues.
> I have an **exciting** job and **the best** colleagues.

	Adjektiv	Komparativ	Superlativ
eine Silbe	*long, big*	*long**er**, big**ger***	*(the) long**est**, big**gest***
zwei Silben mit **-y**	*lucky*	*luck**ier***	*(the) luck**iest***
zwei und mehr Silben	*important*	***more** important*	*(the) **most** important*
unregelmäßig	*good*	*better*	*(the) best*
	bad	*worse*	*(the) worst*

Adjectives and adverbs

G

Adjectives beschreiben Zustände oder Eigenschaften einer Person oder Sache.
Adverbs beschreiben, wie etwas geschieht und beziehen sich meist auf ein Verb oder ein Adjektiv.

	Adjektiv → Adverb
Adjektiv + **-ly**	*quick → quick**ly**; slow → slow**ly***
Adjektiv auf -y > **-ily**	*happy → happ**ily**; easy → eas**ily***
unregelmäßige Adjektive	*good → well; fast → fast; hard → hard; early → early*

G

The *-ing* form of verbs

Um ein Substantiv aus einem Verb zu machen, wird *-ing* hinzugefügt.

I need train**ing** to do the job.
Train**ing** helps you do a better job.

Auf einige Verben folgt *-ing* und auf andere folgt der Infinitiv.

I **enjoy** work**ing** in teams.
He **wants to find** an apprenticeship.

G

Das ***simple past*** wird verwendet, wenn man ausdrücken will, dass etwas zu einem bestimmten Zeitpunkt in der Vergangenheit geschehen ist.
Signalwörter: *yesterday, last … (Monday, week), in … (2019), … (a week) ago*

Das ***present perfect*** wird verwendet, wenn man sagen will, dass etwas geschehen ist oder man drückt damit aus, seit wann oder wie lange ein Zustand schon andauert.
Signalwörter: *just, already, ever, never, (not) yet, lately, recently, for, since*

*I **met** the team in the morning. But I **didn't meet** Niki. I **have just met** her in the cafeteria.*
*I **had** a car accident an hour ago. I**'ve crashed** my mum's new car.*

G

If-sentences Type 1 …

verwendet man, wenn man sagen möchte, was unter bestimmten Bedingungen passiert. Bedingungssätze bestehen aus einem Hauptsatz und einem Nebensatz mit *if*. Typ 1 drückt Bedingungen aus, die leicht erfüllt werden können. Die Folge dieser Bedingung ist wahrscheinlich.

If-Satz: simple present	Hauptsatz: *will*-Futur
*If Mia **stays** at the nursery school,*	*she **will become** a good teacher.*
*If people **stop** helping refugees,*	*they **won't learn** German.*

!

Verwenden Sie nie *will* im *if*-Teil:
If you ~~will~~ want to discuss it, I'll call you.

G

If-sentences Type 2 …

drücken Bedingungen aus, die weniger wahrscheinlich sind. Die Folge dieser Bedingung ist ungewiss.
Bedingungssätze beginnen mit dem *if*-Teil oder dem Hauptsatz. Nach dem *if*-Teil, kommt immer ein Komma.

If-Satz: simple past — Hauptsatz: *would* + Infinitiv
*If we **used** fewer takeaway cups, then we **would** reduce the use of plastic.*

Modal verbs

can/could	*= be able to*	*I* ***can*** *speak English.* (= kann)
may/can	*= be allowed to*	*Beko* ***may*** *visit his cousins in Berlin.* (= dürfen)
may/might	*= perhaps*	*Mia is not here yet. She* ***may*** *be late.* (= wird vielleicht)
must	*= have to*	*They* ***must*** *go to a special class.* (= müssen)
mustn't	*= not allowed to*	*You* ***mustn't*** *forget about their situation.* (= darf nicht)
should/n't	*= ought to*	*Orisa* ***should*** *learn German.* (= sollte)

G

The will future for decisions when you are speaking

Das *will*-Futur wird auch verwendet, wenn etwas im Moment des Sprechens entschieden wird.

Aussage	Verneinung
Can I speak to Ms Schubert, please?	*How about meeting on Friday afternoon?*
– She isn't here now. I ***will*** *ask her to call you back.*	*– OK. I* ***won't*** *plan anything else for then.*

G

The *going to* future …

wird für Absichten und Pläne verwendet.

to meet (treffen)

Aussage	Frage	Verneinung
We ***are going to meet*** *in town.*	***Is*** *Mia* ***going to meet*** *us?*	***I'm not going to meet*** *you.*

G

Relative pronouns …

brauchen Sie, um Personen oder Sachen genauer zu beschreiben.

- *who* wird verwendet, um Personen näher zu beschreiben.

Mia is the friend ***who*** *likes to travel.*

- *which* wird verwendet, um Dinge oder Tiere näher zu beschreiben.

The car ***which*** *Tracy would like to buy is three years old.*

G

!

who und *which* können beide durch *that* ersetzt werden.

Phrases for speaking

Asking about a word or meaning

What does … mean?
How do you say … in English?
I don't understand …
Could you repeat that, please?

Giving your opinion

I think that …
In my opinion …

Asking for an opinion

What do you think about …?
What's your opinion of …?

Agreeing and disagreeing

Yes, I (absolutely) agree.
That's right/true.
You may be right, but …
I don't think that's quite right, because …
Well, I think that …

Saying something in another way

In other words …
What I mean is …

Checking that someone has understood you

Do you see what I mean?
You know what I mean?

Checking that you have understood someone

Do you mean that …?
Really?

Confirming that you have understood something

I see. / Oh, right. / OK then. / Fine.

Asking to speak

Can I just say that …?

Bildquellenverzeichnis

S. 2 PEFC Deutschland e.V.; **S. 5/Jamal** Shutterstock.com / Tutatamafilm; **S. 5/Tracy** Shutterstock.com / Cookie Studio; **S. 5/Mia** Shutterstock.com / Darren Baker; **S. 6/1** Shutterstock.com / juergenhu; **S. 6/2** Shutterstock.com / PhotoPlusProductions; **S. 6/3** Shutterstock.com / Tutti Frutti; **S. 6/4** Shutterstock.com / Dmitry Kalinovsky; **S. 8/ob. li.** Shutterstock.com / Cookie Studio; **S. 8/ob. mi.** Shutterstock.com / Tutatamafilm; **S. 8/ob. re.** Shutterstock.com / Darren Baker; **S. 8/mi. li.** Shutterstock.com / fizkes; **S. 8/mi.** Shutterstock.com / Corepics VOF; **S. 8/mi. re.** Shutterstock.com / goodluz; **S. 10/ob. re.** Shutterstock.com / Rido; **S. 12/mi. re.** Shutterstock.com / Rawpixel.com; **S. 15/1** Shutterstock.com / Monkey Business Images; **S. 15/2** Shutterstock.com / goodluz; **S. 15/3** Shutterstock.com / David Herraez Calzada; **S. 15/4** Shutterstock.com / Kamil Macniak; **S. 15/5** Shutterstock.com / Oksana Kuzmina; **S. 15/6** Shutterstock.com / Rawpixel.com; **S. 15/7** Shutterstock.com / t.max; **S. 15/8** Shutterstock.com / DimiSotirov; **S. 16/un. re.** Shutterstock.com / Jacob Lund; **S. 20/ob. re.** Shutterstock.com / Darren Baker; **S. 23/un. re.** Cornelsen / D'Avila Illustration Agency; **S. 24/ob. li.** Shutterstock.com / kenchiro168; **S. 24/ob. mi.** Shutterstock.com / Monkey Business Images; **S. 24/ob. re.** Shutterstock.com / LightField Studios; **S. 24/mi. li.** Shutterstock.com / bokan; **S. 24/mi.** Shutterstock.com / Adrian Chinery; **S. 24/mi. re.** Shutterstock.com / Lena Pan; **S. 25/ob. re.** Shutterstock.com / Photographee.eu; **S. 25/un. re.** Shutterstock.com / Monkey Business Images; **S. 25/linke Seite** Cornelsen / D'Avila Illustration Agency; **S. 26/mi. re.** Cornelsen / D'Avila Illustration Agency; **S. 29/un. re.** Cornelsen / D'Avila Illustration Agency; **S. 31/un. re.** Shutterstock.com / Anatoliy Karlyuk; **S. 33/ob. re.** Shutterstock.com / Monkey Business Images; **S. 34/ob. re.** Shutterstock.com / Rawpixel.com; **S. 35/1** Shutterstock.com / Kikinunchi; **S. 35/2** Shutterstock.com / ideation90; **S. 35/3** Shutterstock.com / Kzenon; **S. 35/4** Shutterstock.com / PICADORPICTURES; **S. 35/5** Shutterstock.com / Pretty_Pictures; **S. 35/6** Shutterstock.com / M101Studio; **S. 35/ob. re.** Shutterstock.com / Panumas Yanuthai; **S. 35/un. re.** Shutterstock.com / Matej Kastelic; **S. 37/ob. li.** Cornelsen / D'Avila Illustration Agency; **S. 38/un. re.** Shutterstock.com / Darren Baker; **S. 39/mi. li.** Shutterstock.com / Yulia Glam; **S. 40/ob. li.** Shutterstock.com / Monkey Business Images; **S. 40/mi. re.** Shutterstock.com / wavebreakmedia; **S. 40/un. li.** Shutterstock.com / Mick Russell; **S. 42/mi. re.** Shutterstock.com / Monkey Business Images; **S. 43/ob. re.** Shutterstock.com / pixelheadphoto digitalskillet; **S. 44/ob. li.** Shutterstock.com / JARIRIYAWAT; **S. 44/ob. re.** Shutterstock.com / MaxShutter; **S. 44/ob. mi.** Shutterstock.com / TRMK; **S. 45/A** Shutterstock.com / Anna Suslina; **S. 45/B** Shutterstock.com / Fascinadora; **S. 45/C** Shutterstock.com / Egrigorovich; **S. 45/D** Shutterstock.com / Anna Rogalska; **S. 45/E** Shutterstock.com / rarrarorro; **S. 45/F** Shutterstock.com / Kira Budaieva; **S. 45/ob. re.** Shutterstock.com / Flystock; **S. 45/un. re.** Shutterstock.com / Fedor Konoplin; **S. 46/Emojis** Shutterstock.com / Igillustrator; **S. 48/ob. li.** © Fairtrade Deutschland; **S. 48/ob. re.** © Global Organic Textile Standard; GOTS; **S. 48/2. v. li.** FOREST STEWARDSHIP COUNCIL® (FSC®); **S. 48/3. v. li.** © RAL gGmbH; **S. 49/un. re.** Shutterstock.com / Olkita; **S. 50/1-8** Cornelsen / D'Avila Illustration Agency; **S. 52/alle** Cornelsen / D'Avila Illustration Agency; **S. 53/alle** Cornelsen / D'Avila Illustration Agency; **S. 54/A-C** Cornelsen / D'Avila Illustration Agency; **S. 55/ob. re.** Shutterstock.com / maximino; **S. 55/un. re.** Shutterstock.com / William Perugini; **S. 55/1-6** Cornelsen / D'Avila Illustration Agency; **S. 56/ob. re.** Shutterstock.com / Monkey Business Images; **S. 59/mi. re.** Shutterstock.com / Nomad_Soul; **S. 61/ob. re.** Shutterstock.com / Pensee Sauvage; **S. 63/1** Shutterstock.com / petch one; **S. 63/2** Shutterstock.com / vallustrationstudio; **S. 63/3** Shutterstock.com / LDDesign; **S. 63/4** Shutterstock.com / Aquene Ardeen; **S. 63/5** Shutterstock.com / Prokopenko Oleg; **S. 63/6** Shutterstock.com / awang_79; **S. 64/ob. re.** Shutterstock.com / garetsworkshop; **S. 64/un.** Cornelsen / D'Avila Illustration Agency; **S. 65/ob. re.** Shutterstock.com / Iakov Filimonov; **S. 65/A** Shutterstock.com / mimagephotography; **S. 65/B** Shutterstock.com / Monkey Business Images; **S. 65/C** Shutterstock.com / GaudiLab; **S. 65/un. re.** Shutterstock.com / Jacob Lund; **S. 66/mi. re.** Shutterstock.com / Peter Hermes Furian; **S. 68/A-C** Cornelsen / D'Avila Illustration Agency; **S. 68/un. li.** Shutterstock.com / Alexey Boldin; **S. 68/un. mi.** Shutterstock.com / sockagphoto; **S. 70/li.** Shutterstock.com / Weekend Warrior Photos; **S. 70/re.** Shutterstock.com / karamysh; **S. 70/mi.** Shutterstock.com / turtix; **S. 73/mi.** Shutterstock.com / Andrey_Popov; **S. 74/ob. mi.** Shutterstock.com / I Wei Huang; **S. 75/ob. re.** Shutterstock.com / Stuart Miles; **S. 75/un. re.** Shutterstock.com / Foxxy63; **S. 75/li.** Cornelsen / D'Avila Illustration Agency; **S. 76/ob. re.** Shutterstock.com / Sasun Bughdaryan; **S. 78/A** Shutterstock.com / Robert Kneschke; **S. 78/B** Shutterstock.com / AndriyShevchuk; **S. 78/C** Shutterstock.com / Sorbis; **S. 78/D** Shutterstock.com / GaudiLab; **S. 80/ob. re.** Shutterstock.com / Monkey Business Images; **S. 85/un. li.** Shutterstock.com / Iva Vagnerova; **S. 86/3.1** Shutterstock.com / Mr.Timoty; **S. 86/3.2** Shutterstock.com / Neil Carrington; **S. 86/3.3** Shutterstock.com / everydayplus; **S. 86/3.4** Shutterstock.com / Andrey_Popov; **S. 86/3.5** Shutterstock.com / Tero Vesalainen; **S. 86/3.6** Shutterstock.com / Josep Suria; **S. 86/4.1** Shutterstock.com / Omelnytskyi; **S. 86/4.2** Shutterstock.com / Aniwhite; **S. 86/4.3** Shutterstock.com / ALPA PROD; **S. 86/4.4** Shutterstock.com / michaeljung; **S. 86/4.5** Shutterstock.com / Skumer; **S. 86/4.6** Shutterstock.com / fizkes; **S. 87/A** Shutterstock.com / Rawpixel.com; **S. 87/B** Shutterstock.com / Inside Creative House; **S. 87/C** Shutterstock.com / Libor Pî?ka; **S. 87/D** Shutterstock.com / Oleksiy Mark; **S. 87/E** Shutterstock.com / ViDI Studio; **S. 87/F** Shutterstock.com / Andrey_Popov; **S. 89** Cornelsen / D'Avila Illustration Agency; **S. 92** Cornelsen / D'Avila Illustration Agency; **S. 100/Emojis** Cornelsen / D'Avila Illustration Agency; **S. 122** Cornelsen / Carlos Borrell